Bitcoin Widow

Jennifer Robertson

WITH STEPHEN KIMBER

Bitcoin Widow

Love, Betrayal and the Missing Millions

HarperCollins*Publishers*Ltd

Bitcoin Widow
Copyright © 2022 by Jennifer Robertson.
All rights reserved.

Published by HarperCollins Publishers Ltd

First edition

HarperCollins books may be purchased for educational, business or sales
promotional use through our Special Markets Department.

HarperCollins Publishers Ltd
Bay Adelaide Centre, East Tower
22 Adelaide Street West, 41st Floor
Toronto, Ontario, Canada
M5H 4E3

www.harpercollins.ca

Library and Archives Canada Cataloguing in Publication

Title: Bitcoin widow : love, betrayal and the missing millions / Jennifer
Robertson; with Stephen Kimber. Names: Robertson, Jennifer (Jennifer Kathleen
Margaret), author. | Kimber, Stephen, author. Description: First edition.
Identifiers: Canadiana (print) 20210340479 | Canadiana (ebook) 20210340967
| ISBN 9781443463904 (softcover) | ISBN 9781443463911 (ebook)
Subjects: LCSH: Robertson, Jennifer (Jennifer Kathleen Margaret) | LCSH:
Bitcoin—Canada. | LCSH: Business failures—Canada. | LCSH: Bankruptcy—
Canada. | LCGFT: Autobiographies. Classification: LCC HG3769.C34 R63
2022 | DDC 332.7/50971—dc23

Printed and bound in the United States of America

LSC/C 9 8 7 6 5 4 3 2 1

To my family and friends, for their unwavering and unconditional love and support.

You can't go back and change the beginning, but you can start where you are and change the ending. —C.S. Lewis

Contents

Prologue

His face was pale, whiter than I'd ever seen. I'd been unpacking my suitcase, trying to choose a dress to wear to dinner, when I looked over and saw Gerry lying on the bed in our hotel room, his face contorted in pain, his hands gripping at the side of the bed.

"Oh my God, are you OK?"

"I don't know," he said. I'd never heard Gerry say "I don't know" before. That wasn't Gerry. He was stoic when it came to his stomach pain. Usually it would be just "Yeah, I'm fine."

"I don't know," he repeated, with a moan this time. It was around 6:30 in the evening on December 8, 2018, and we'd only recently checked in to our hotel in Jaipur, India.

"Is the pain from Crohn's, or from food poisoning?" I asked. Gerry had had frequent bouts of serious stomach pain since he was a teenager and had been diagnosed with Crohn's disease, an inflammatory bowel disease that causes inflammation in the digestive tract, when he was twenty-four. In the four years we'd been together, he'd had occasional, painful flare-ups. At one point, he considered surgery, but his doctor prescribed steroids instead that seemed to ease his suffering. "Your medicine is going to be expensive," the doctor told him, "so you'd better make a lot of money." Gerry had.

Gerry had begun to feel ill that afternoon just before we boarded our flight from Varanasi, also in India, to Jaipur. "I think the Indian food got me," he'd joked. "My stomach really hurts." We'd eaten lunch at the Dolphin, a recently opened restaurant on the banks of the Ganges River. As usual, Gerry had done his research in advance, checking the reviews and making sure there were no complaints about the food. He'd had no complaints, either—at the time. He told me his rice and meat dish was very good. As for me, I also felt fine, but I knew it could still be food poisoning. We'd travelled enough and had too many experiences with bad food. Just the week before, in fact, we'd been vacationing in the Bahamas with our friends when Gerry suddenly announced he needed to go to our room because his stomach hurt "crazy bad." He was gone for a couple of hours, and told me later he'd thrown up his lunch.

But he'd never looked as awful as this.

"Do you need to go to the hospital?" I asked.

"No," he said. "I'll just wait for a bit, see if I feel better."

And that was that.

IN OUR RELATIONSHIP, Gerry always had the last word. He was extremely intelligent, so I took what he said as the final say. That hadn't been true in any of my past relationships. During my first marriage, I had been the one working more than one job to cover our expenses while taking care of our home and dog, and I made all the important decisions about our life together. That didn't work out so well. By the time Jacob and I had split, I ended up with crippling debt.

So I took comfort in letting someone I trusted—and I trusted Gerry completely—make decisions. To be honest, I also knew our money—wealth I'd never dreamed of while growing up in Nova Scotia—came from Gerry's work. That wasn't totally true now. In the past two years, I'd built Robertson Nova, our residential property management company, from nothing into a financial success. But I also knew that without Gerry's capital, I would not have had my company. I appreciated the opportunities Gerry had given me, but, partly because he had done so, I never felt like I was in charge.

Tonight, I simply accepted his decision to wait, cancelled our reservations in the hotel restaurant and ordered room service and a few DVDs for us to watch later. While we waited for them to arrive, I decided I would have a bath.

Gerry and I were on what was supposed to be an extended honeymoon. We'd gotten legally married six months earlier, on June 8, 2018, in the backyard of our house on Kinross Court in Fall River, a suburb of Halifax. The ceremony itself was short and sweet—just two friends and a justice of the peace. After nearly four years together, we'd simply decided it was time to make it official.

My dream wedding, with both our families present, took place a few months later, at a stunning castle in Scotland rented just for the occasion. Another gift from Gerry. After that, we'd enjoyed a mini-honeymoon, a few days in Amsterdam, but we still wanted to celebrate the occasion with an amazing honeymoon adventure. Just the two of us. The year before, Gerry and I had taken a Christmas cruise around South America. We loved the leisurely experience of cruising, as well as being away over Christmas. I came from a broken family, meaning the usual rounds of family holiday dinners and visits with different factions of family were inevitably exhausting and best avoided. Largely because of that, Gerry and I had already decided our honeymoon would include another Christmas cruise. Although we were both keen travellers, planning our itineraries was always my responsibility. I booked us on a cruise leaving Auckland, New Zealand, in the middle of December and arriving in Sydney, Australia, two days before its famous New Year's Eve fireworks.

India was a stopover with a purpose. Back in February, Gerry and I had gone through a *Shark Tank* craze. Gerry liked business reality TV shows because he was a numbers guy, but *Shark Tank*, the American version of *Dragons' Den*, appealed to me as well because of all the uplifting human stories. On one of the programs we watched together, we saw a segment about a Texas couple whose premature baby had died. They decided to honour her memory by using the profits from their very successful company to build orphanages in India, working with an organization called Angel House.

The idea intrigued me. I'd always been interested in international development, though I'd never imagined I would have enough money to finance an orphanage. But in the last two years, Quadriga, Gerry's company, had become incredibly successful. We had more money than we needed. Why not? I did extensive research on the charity, talked to the founder of Angel House and felt comfortable our money would be well spent. Gerry agreed. My hope was that this would be the beginning of a new charitable chapter in our lives. We had done so well and enjoyed so much; it was time to begin to give back. We paid $21,000 (US) to have Angel House construct a twelve-child orphanage in India. We didn't get to pick where it would be or have any influence over any other details, just what it would be called, what the plaque would say and whether we wanted to purchase a drinking well with it. We did.

We arranged to attend the official opening of the "Jennifer Robertson and Gerald Cotten Home for Orphaned Children" on December 13 in Venkatapuram, an hour's drive from Hyderabad, the next stop on our journey through India. I'd brought along twelve teddy bears, one for each child at the orphanage.

We left Canada at the end of November, flying first class to New Delhi. The next day, we hired a car for the three-hour journey to Agra, an ancient city that, along with Delhi and Jaipur, is part of what they call India's Golden Triangle of tourist attractions. I'd booked us a three-night stay at the Oberoi Amarvilas, a massive, palatial, five-star luxury hotel filled with gourmet restaurants, spas, fountains, terraced lawns, reflection pools and pavilions, all hidden behind huge gates to keep the chaotic city of a million and a half people at bay.

One evening, we went to see a show—the love story behind the building of the famous Taj Mahal, a UNESCO World Heritage Site that is known as "the jewel of Muslim art in India"—and Gerry uncharacteristically decided we should walk from the hotel through the streets to get there. It was early evening and already dark. The streets were teeming with people, cows, motorbikes and cars going off in all directions. I'll admit I was nervous that we might be hit by something. But Gerry, who usually loathed crowds, was cool as a cucumber.

For me, the most memorable moment from our time in Agra was the night we had a private dinner on the balcony of our hotel room, which overlooked the Taj Mahal. The white marble mausoleum silhouetted against the purple and orange night sky was stunning.

On December 4, we drove back to New Delhi and then flew to Varanasi, a sacred city. I'd chosen Varanasi for a four-day stopover because I wanted to see the Ganges River and better understand its religious significance. I was especially intrigued to visit the spot where the Buddha is said to have offered his first sermon. I had majored in religious studies in university and had always been interested in religious and historical sites around the world.

We stayed at the BrijRama Palace on the banks of the Ganges; to get there, we had to travel up the river by boat. We arrived in the evening, and I was in complete awe: so many people with no apparent order, people cooking on fires at the side of the main road. I told Gerry it seemed almost apocalyptic.

Because our hotel was located on the banks of the Ganges, it didn't serve alcohol. Local Hindu priests consider consuming alcohol or mutton near the holy river a "sacrilege." Despite the fact we would only be at the hotel for four nights, Gerry made sure to bring along his own quart of vodka. On our last night, I asked if I could have a drink, my first since we arrived, and he told me he'd already finished the whole bottle. I was shocked. I hadn't seen him drinking. "How did you drink the whole bottle?" I asked, my voice rising with concern. Although we both enjoyed alcohol, I'd noticed Gerry seemed to be drinking more heavily since a Crohn's flare-up in June, even though he knew drinking was a trigger for Crohn's attacks. So was stress. And Gerry was stressed, too. There were money issues he didn't like to talk about, including a problem with CIBC that I understood had led to the freezing of millions of dollars in one of Quadriga's accounts. Although I knew I should confront him about his drinking—for his own health—I kept putting off that discussion for another day.

Was that the real reason his stomach hurt so badly now?

* * *

INDIA WASN'T GERRY'S IDEA. It was mine. And not just because of the orphanage. Although I'd grown up in a Nova Scotia that was still mostly white in a family with zero interest in foreign destinations, I was—for reasons I cannot explain to you now—passionate about travel, obsessed with dreams of experiencing worlds beyond the only one I'd known. By the time I was in my teens, I routinely pored over the latest issues of *National Geographic* and travel magazines with an almost religious fervour, creating my own checklists of countries to visit.

I credit Mehek, my smart, motivated, funny Toronto best friend, with kindling my particular desire to visit India. Mehek, who is a few years younger than me, was born in Mumbai and immigrated with her family to Toronto when she was in her late teens. We met there when we briefly worked together as the only employees at an awful temporary staffing business. We commiserated over our unhappiness with our jobs and bonded over our desire to travel. Mehek often shared stories that were exotic to me of growing up in India, a country she said she wanted to return to someday. Her mother would sometimes invite me to their house for dosas—crispy, savoury Indian pancakes—and conversations about India that only made me keener to see the country.

Before Gerry and I moved in together in May 2015, while we were still in that stage of sharing all our dreams and hopes for the future, I told him, "One day, I want to visit India."

India, it turned out, was the one country in the whole world Gerry never wanted to visit. "Why would you ever want to go to India?" he shot back. "There's, like, a bajillion people there." It was one of our few disagreements, and the only one about travel.

If my reasons for wanting to go were gauzy and coloured by my imagination, Gerry's reasons for not wanting to were clear. He was a germaphobe. He was obsessively concerned about his food, and not just because his immune system had been compromised by Crohn's. He had this "don't-touch-this, don't-eat-that" mentality. He wouldn't allow his hands to touch his food. He even ate popcorn with a skewer! Except . . . candy. Gerry was also a candyholic who could never seem to sate his sweet tooth; sometimes, he'd even skip dinner and just eat candy instead. Gummy bears, the small, gelatin-based, fruit-flavoured gum candies, were his absolute favourites. And yet he wouldn't eat leftovers if they were two days old because he was concerned they wouldn't be safe.

So it was no surprise that India, with its overcrowding and poverty, had never made Gerry's bucket list.

I'd told him I would go and open the orphanage myself. I'm a seasoned traveller. But Gerry said, "No. I'll come." We had this running joke after that, that I had to open an orphanage to get him to come with me to India. Gerry was always supportive, but the orphanage was never an idea he cared much about. To make India more appealing to him, I booked us into the best hotels, and we ate out only in the best restaurants.

But now Gerry was lying on the bed, in the worst pain I'd ever seen. Was it something he ate? A wave of panic washed over me. It was my fault we were in India . . . my fault he was ill.

OUR PLAN had been to spend a few days wandering around the Pink City, as Jaipur is known, visiting the Galtaji temple complex and its monkey colonies. I'd even booked us a hot-air balloon tour of the city, one of our favourite pastimes on our travels. After that, we would fly to Hyderabad, open the orphanage and then head on to Auckland and our honeymoon cruise!

We landed in Jaipur around 5 p.m. Our hotel, the Oberoi Rajvilas, sent a luxury SUV and two people dressed in formal sherwani long jackets and baggy Punjabi pants to pick us up at the airport. The Oberoi was beautiful, with amazing service, above and beyond the nicest hotel I'd ever experienced, and by that point, I had experienced a lot of cool places. Staff brought us to our room, which was more like a private villa with a canopied four-poster bed and a view of our own private court-yard. The first thing we noticed when we walked in was a sign on the dresser that spelled out C-O-N-G-R-A-T-S in carefully arranged yellow flower petals—we'd told the hotel we were on our honeymoon. Staff had already prepared a rose-petal bath in the sunken marble tub.

I had only been in the bath for a few minutes, but I couldn't relax. I was anxious. Gerry often had stomach issues, but the pain had never seemed this bad, never lasted this long.

I thought, *I need to make sure he's OK.*

So I stepped out of the bath and walked into the room, where he was lying on the bed. His face was now as white as the cotton sheets on our bed, and his skin was clammy to the touch.

"OK, I don't care what you say," I told him, definite this time. "You're going to the hospital." It was the first time I'd ever taken charge like that.

He didn't say anything at first and then just "OK."

I picked up the phone and called the hotel's front desk.

1

Swipe Right

I've always thought of myself as an adventure junkie, someone who delights in exploring new places, learning new things,
trying on new experiences. When I was in high school, I believed
I was destined to lead an extraordinary life. "If my life turns out
to be ordinary," I would repeat to myself over and over, almost as
a mantra, "I'll just die."

I'm not sure I would say the same, or even close, today, but the
reality is that my real life before I met Gerry was relatively ordinary, certainly not the stuff of the breathless international head-
lines it became.

I was born Jennifer Kathleen Margaret Griffith. There are two
things you may want to know about that. The first is that there

are eight letters in each of my names, and—since I was also born on January 28, 1988, at 8:02 a.m.—the number eight has played an outsized role in my life. I used to believe the number eight represented a positive omen. When I married my first husband, for example, I decided it was meant to be, in part, because his last name also had eight letters. I made sure our official exchange of vows even occurred on the eighth day of February in 2012. In the end, that marriage didn't turn out so well. Neither have other significant life moments with eight in them. Gerry was admitted to the hospital in India on December 8, 2018.

The second thing you should know is that I never liked my last name, Griffith. To me, the name never felt elegant, never sounded pretty in my head. After my parents divorced, my only connection to that name—my father—no longer connected. That was one reason I was so keen to change my name when I married Jacob Forgeron. But then I became Forgeron without Jacob, and that name didn't feel like mine, either. All that may seem unimportant in the larger scheme of things—and it is—but after my divorce from Jacob and before I married Gerry, I legally changed my last name to Robertson. Robertson? I'll explain later how and why I chose that name—and why it mattered—but suffice it to say, it mattered to a lot of people.

* * *

My parents came from very different life experiences. My mother, Carol, was the daughter of an alcoholic. She grew up with nine brothers and sisters in a trailer park in Dartmouth, Nova Scotia, and became pregnant with her own first child when she was seventeen. By the time she met my father, she'd already had two children and was in the midst of divorcing her first husband. She was looking to buy a car, and my father was looking to sell her one.

By contrast, my father, Dale, and his twin sister, Debbie, grew up in a relatively stable middle-class family in Bedford, a suburb of Halifax. My father followed his father into the car sales business. Some of my dad's older clients, he once told me, had actually purchased their first cars from *his* father. That probably tells you all you need to know about the small-town community in which I grew up.

My parents married in 1987. By the time I came along, my mother was thirty-five, my half-sister, Kim, was seventeen and my half-brother, Adam, was fourteen. Given the differences in our ages, they acted more like caregivers than siblings. Kim became my frequent babysitter, even more often after she had her own daughter, Amanda, when I was five. Amanda and I grew up together, more sisters than aunt and niece. Adam doted on me. When I was little, he would spend his own money to buy me dresses and was always in the front row for any of my important life events: school graduations, piano recitals, dance recitals. Even after Adam moved out and got on with his own life, and we didn't talk to each other on a regular basis, he would pop back into my life whenever I needed him—without me having to ask.

Growing up, we were never poor, as my mother had been, but we certainly weren't rich, either. My father sold cars on commission; some years, he did well, but there would be stretches—sometimes as long as half a year at a time—when he didn't bring home a penny. My mother was a shift worker at the post office. We lived paycheque to paycheque. Occasionally, my parents would even remortgage our house just to try to balance the books that never seemed to balance.

That said, my parents always assumed I would go to university, and they made sure I had the funding I would need for that by signing up for an education savings plan when I was very young. By the time I graduated high school, they had put aside enough for my first two and a half years of university tuition.

Nothing of significance seems to have happened in my own life until I started junior high—except perhaps this: when I was very young, my parents moved to my dad's family cottage on a large lake in a rural community half an hour from Bedford. They relocated there year-round to see if they preferred country living.

They put their house in Bedford up for sale, but it didn't sell. So, three years later, we moved back to Bedford. Why was it significant? I'll come back to that.

In September 2000, I began Grade 7 at Bedford Junior High School and met the three girls who would become my closest women friends. I can't tell you exactly why we connected, but I do know it began when Afton, who was a cousin of one of my elementary school friends, invited me to hang out at her house after school one day. I was thrilled she'd invited me, even more so when I met her two best friends, Aly and Anne, and became best friends with them, too. Aly, Anne and I very quickly became inseparable. We've been through absolutely everything together since.

We were never what I would call "bad kids," but during the first years of our friendship, we discovered the suburban teenage joys of girlfriends, boys, parties and alcohol. My mother, who'd grown up having to take care of her two younger sisters, was eager for me to have the childhood she'd never had. She encouraged me to be adventurous, though she probably never intended any of the adventures that followed.

Because my parents let me live in our finished basement, which had a walkout to the backyard, my house quickly became our group's gathering place. We would have sleepovers, sneaking out in the middle of the night to meet other kids, drink and party.

That's how I met Jacob. Afton and I encountered him one night while wandering the neighbourhood. He was very drunk. I complained to Afton later: "Man, that Jacob guy was so annoying. Wasn't he annoying? I can't stand that guy." But then I met him again when he wasn't so drunk, and he wasn't so annoying. I also discovered he was turning nineteen. "You can buy us liquor," I told him. And he did. For all of us. It wasn't such a big deal. In my neighbourhood, older kids often bought alcohol for those who were underage. Jacob would come by my house in his car. "We're just going out for a drive," I'd tell my parents. We'd go to the liquor store and buy booze—usually big coolers, or Colt 45 beers, sometimes vodka—come back, and I'd sneak the bottles into the house in my purse.

Jacob and I became friends and then more. He was the first person I ever slept with. It happened during March break in Grade 10. He was nineteen and already working full time. My sixteen-year-old heart said, "I love you." His man-boy response was "Oh God . . . yeah, OK . . ." And then we didn't see each other again for three years!

During junior high, my grades, which had never even been an issue in elementary school, began to slip, thanks in part to the fact I'd begun French immersion in junior high. It had seemed like a good idea at the time, but trying to learn new concepts in math—

never my strong suit—in a new language convinced me to switch back to the English stream in Grade 9. My grades improved. I did well enough at Charles P. Allen High School to earn small entrance scholarships to Mount Saint Vincent University and Saint Mary's University, both of which were local. I didn't apply to universities elsewhere because I knew the money my parents had saved for me would last longer if I lived at home, and I ultimately chose Mount Saint Vincent, the women's university, mostly because it was closer to our house than Saint Mary's, which was located at the far southern end of the Halifax peninsula.

My stay-at-home plan didn't survive my first year.

To begin with, Jacob came back into my life. He'd moved out to British Columbia for work, but returned to Halifax around the time of my high school graduation. I'd heard through the grapevine he was back, but I also learned he had returned with a girlfriend, so I didn't even try to get in touch. Besides, I'd just been through my own bad breakup after a three-year relationship.

But then, in November 2007, Jacob added me as a Facebook friend. He and his girlfriend had split up. She'd returned out west, and so Jacob and I started talking. Then we began going out on dates. Well, not "going out," exactly. We'd order sushi, enjoy a bottle of wine and watch an episode of *House*. We began hanging out together all the time, became best friends, called each other soulmates, fell back in love. Truth? I'd never stopped loving him, but this time I made sure to wait for him to say the "I love you" first. And he did. We talked about moving in together.

The timing turned out to be ideal; my parents had been patiently waiting for me to move out so they, too, could move out—each on their own. I'd known since junior high school that my parents weren't getting along. When I was in high school, they began sleeping in separate bedrooms. At some point, my mother began seeing a co-worker named Tom Beazley, who would become my stepfather.

Some of my girlfriends who knew what was going on were worried for me. "Aren't you upset?" they asked.

I wasn't. "My parents have been so unhappy for so long," I told them, "I just truly want them both to be happy."

Besides, I was ready to begin my own life. And not just with Jacob.

"OK," I DECLARED, "I want to go to Greece. Who wants to come with me?"

It was the winter of my first year of university, and I had decided, after seeing some stunning photos of Greece—those cliff-hugging villages filled with white-painted stone houses highlighted by those blue doors and windows the colour of the Greek flag, complemented by pink bougainvillea flowers, all set against the eternal blue of Mediterranean sea and sky—I had to see the place for myself. It would be one modest baby step in my determination to lead that extraordinary life. (While I was in high school, I'd also gone on a week-long school trip to France and immediately put Paris on my see-again list.)

I'm not sure where my wanderlust came from. Certainly not from my parents. The very idea of travel still makes my mother, who is anxious to start with, even more so. And while my dad will say he likes "anywhere warm," he's never expressed any interest in going somewhere different or seeing anything new.

Aly and Anne, however, were up for an end-of-first-year-of-university adventure. We found Contiki, a group travel packaging company that specializes in social tours for young people aged eighteen to thirty-five. We signed up for a whirlwind month-long London-to-Athens-and-Corfu adventure. We mostly slept in hostels, had adventures, made new friends. Because I have dark brown hair, Aly has bright red hair and Anne is a platinum blonde, we became known among our new friends as "Charlie's Angels" after the series of crime/action films of the early 2000s. It was exhausting and exhilarating, and, even before it ended, I couldn't wait to do it again.

The trip was expensive—around $8,000 each, including air-fare—but worth every penny. I was lucky. Although my parents had taken care of most of my tuition worries, I'd also been working part time since I was sixteen and landed my first after-school job at our local Tim Hortons. I'd quickly graduated to Winners, the off-price department store, and then, soon after I turned nineteen, became a bartender and waitress at the Old Port Pub and Grill, a busy pub in an industrial park in Dartmouth where I could work as many hours as I could squeeze in and where I earned more in tips than I could have made in most full-time jobs.

Long before I met Gerry, I understood the importance of being financially independent.

JACOB AND I had to navigate more than a few relationship speed bumps on the way to moving in together. In the fall of 2007, he announced he would be going on the road for four months, helping open new stores across the country for his employer. Long-distance love didn't work out well, certainly not from my point of view. After having been inseparable, best friends, soul-mates and all the rest for more than nine months, he simply disappeared from my life, didn't communicate and didn't seem to want anything to do with me. I was heartbroken.

But then he returned near the end of November, we got back together and Jacob moved into my parents' house with me because of his own problems at home. His dad had Alzheimer's disease and his mother, who was battling cancer, had had to sell the family house for financial reasons. But then, just two days before Christmas, I came home from work to find that Jacob had moved all his stuff out of the house.

I called him. "What the hell?"

"Yeah, I don't want to be with you." That was all.

I was devastated. On Christmas Eve, my friend Aly came over to commiserate. She brought a joint, and we smoked it on the balcony. My mother, who was very much against drugs, didn't even object.

Less than two months later, however, Jacob and I were back together. And by Halloween we had finally moved into our own apartment in Clayton Park, a suburb near Mount Saint Vincent, where our couple lives seemed to settle into something resembling stability.

When I began at Mount Saint Vincent, I officially enrolled as a bachelor of arts student, but I took a lot of business courses. I even considered switching to a bachelor of business administration program, but changed my mind when I realized I would have to spend an extra year in school to get my degree. I wasn't *that* interested! Instead, I became the only person in my 2011 graduating class to earn a BA with a major in religious studies and a minor in business.

It was my sister, Kim, who suggested I try some religious studies courses, which she told me she'd found fascinating when she was a student. She was right. For me, the courses also fed my desire to discover a larger world beyond the Bedford of my growing up. Geography had been one of my favourite courses in high school, and religious studies expanded my horizons. I learned so much in those courses about different peoples and their histories, cultures and beliefs, and it fed my desire to experience all those places for myself.

At some point, I even explored the idea of a career in international development. I imagined myself travelling the world as a field worker for an organization like World Vision, the international Christian charity. But I quickly discovered most international development fieldwork jobs paid very little—compared even with the tips I earned as a bartender—and most positions that did interest me required a master's degree. Still, in the process of exploring the web pages of international development organizations, I realized that those who did their hiring earned significantly more than those they hired. What if . . . ?

I discovered a one-year certificate program in human resources at McMaster University in Hamilton, Ontario, applied and was accepted. My theory was that if I could find my way into an HR job with an international development agency, I could use that as a springboard to a dream job in the field. Naive, I realize now, but it made sense to me at the time.

In September 2011, Jacob and I moved to Ontario. Jacob, who'd been working for a national auto parts and equipment retailer, simply transferred to its Hamilton outlet to train as a manager, with full benefits and a pension to look forward to. I found part-time work as a bartender and waitress at Tailgate Charlie's, a sports bar and restaurant in Hamilton that offered me as many hours as I could handle between classes. We were far better off financially than many of our friends, most of whom were still struggling with college debt while they tried to figure out what they wanted to do with the rest of their lives.

Jacob told me he already knew what he wanted to do with the rest of his life: he wanted to get married and start a family. Why not? We were in love. I was about to graduate with my HR certificate in April 2012. What could go wrong?

We officially exchanged our vows in front of a justice of the peace in Brantford, Ontario, on February 8, 2012. While it was a very low-key event—my mom flew in from Halifax, one of Jacob's co-workers attended as well—we had already decided that our real celebration, a week-long party of awesomeness with forty of our best friends and family, would take place three months later at the Majestic Colonial resort in the Dominican Republic. Aly and Anne agreed to be bridesmaids. My dream was that we would have the wedding on May 8—eight again!—but someone else had already booked the resort's wedding facilities for that day, so we had to settle for May 7. I consoled myself with the fact that the eighth would be the first full day of our married life.

The wedding week was everything I'd hoped—the resort was beautiful, the accommodations perfect, the party the best—but when it was over, I suddenly came face to face with the daunting reality that I needed to find a job in human resources—and immediately. The problem was that I had just graduated and had no experience to leverage into the kind of responsible position I hoped for. The job I eventually found—essentially as a recruiter for a high-paced temporary staffing agency—was based in Toronto, an hour-and-a-half commute each way from Hamilton. The job itself was stressful. I was always dealing with some new crisis: we'd promised to send five people to a client, and three hadn't shown up for work. I'd be on the phone at six in the morning, calling random people to replace them. To make matters worse, the skill set the job required was way out of my comfort zone. It was a sales job, something I'd never done before. I had to find companies to sell our services to, then recruit people to do work for them. It turned out I wasn't very good at selling or recruiting. Worst of all, the job paid just $15 an hour. I made far less than I'd been earning at Tailgate Charlie's working only part time.

The only positive about the job was meeting Mehek.

Jacob? Unlike me, he was happy enough to spend his days at his job, then come home and play video games. He expressed little interest in helping with the household chores or caring for Nitro, the chihuahua I'd bought in 2006 when we first talked of moving in together. I called him Nitro because he was such a small dog; I wanted to give him a big, powerful name. He's been my best buddy ever since.

The only other good news—or so I thought at the time—was that I had my weekends off for the first time since I'd begun bartending. We became friends with one of Jacob's co-workers and her boyfriend. They were older than we were—she was about forty, he was thirty—and they had a child together, but we hit it off, hanging out at their house every weekend. She and I would walk our dogs together; sometimes she'd take care of Nitro for us.

But after a while I began to wonder about Jacob's relationship with her. Nothing specific, just intuition. When I'd raise concerns—"You two seem to be a little too close, and it's making me uncomfortable"—Jacob would get angry and defensive, insisting nothing was going on. It all came to a head one Saturday morning in May 2013, just a week before our first anniversary. We had scheduled an appointment that day to meet with a mortgage broker. Houses were incredibly cheap in Hamilton at the time, so we'd decided it was time to take the next step on our life path and buy a house on the way to having children and living happily ever after.

But I couldn't help myself. Jacob was still asleep. His phone was on the computer desk. I felt a pull, almost physical, to check it out. I picked it up, scrolled through his text messages, and there it was. A message he'd neglected to delete:

> [He] I love you.
> [She] I wish I knew how much you love me.
> [He] I love you so much.

I woke him up. We had a big fight. It turned out he'd been having the affair with the co-worker—a woman I'd thought of as my friend—for six months. Still, he begged me to stay, said he didn't want a divorce, didn't want to be with her and wanted nothing more than to stay with me.

For reasons that seemed to make sense to me at the time, if no longer, I eventually agreed to try again. We stopped seeing his co-worker, and Jacob transferred to a part-time position at another outlet in Mississauga. He also applied to a civil engineering technology program at Humber College in Etobicoke. "You can do this," I told him, and I was sure he could. Jacob was far smarter than he'd ever allowed himself to be. We moved, too, to an apartment on the border between Toronto and Etobicoke, near a GO train station and just five minutes from my job. It felt like opening a new chapter. Everything was good again.

That wasn't totally true. Moving from Hamilton to Toronto meant our rent doubled, so we were struggling again financially. I'd gone back to bartending on the side, working as many hours as I could handle at Wild Wing, a sports bar and restaurant chain. But I was unhappy, and I let him know.

But then, in November 2013, I landed the most incredible job at a huge marketing agency just up the street from my previous position. Initially, I was hired on as a temporary recruiter, but the pay was $22 an hour. Two months later, they offered me a six-month contract as the HR administrator for a team working for a cellphone shop owned by a national supermarket chain. I took the position with the understanding it would likely become permanent. It wasn't just a job; it was the best job ever. I'd walk in each morning and have no idea what to expect. Some days, I'd be walking around the office and see an old-fashioned popcorn machine.

"Popcorn?" someone would ask. Sure. I'd go downstairs, and there would always be a huge stack of every single chocolate bar you could ever imagine. We went out for lunch all the time. Our boss didn't fret. "Yeah, just take a few hours off," he'd say.

It was too good to last, and it didn't. Two-thirds of the way through the contract, I arrived at work one morning to discover all our company email addresses had been shut down. The super-market chain had decided to drop our marketing agency as its pro-vider, and that was that. Although I was kept on by the marketing company, it was clear there would be no long-term job security.

Jacob and I talked it over. Even though our relationship hadn't improved much since his affair, I still believed I was in love with him. I was prepared to do whatever it took to fix our marriage. In similar circumstances, some couples have a baby; we decided to go on a backpacking adventure in Southeast Asia. We planned it together, Jacob as excited as I to experience a world we'd only heard about. I was keen to visit every one of the amazing temples I'd read about in my religious studies courses. I was only twenty-six; we had no kids and no debt. My bartending savings had long since paid for our $20,000 destination wedding.

When Jacob quit his job, he walked away with a profit-sharing payout of close to $10,000, thanks to having spent a decade with the same company. After we came home, he was confident they would hire him back part time while he finished his Humber program. Although I would be leaving my now-tenuous contract job at the marketing company, I too had no doubt I could find work when we returned, either in HR or, at least for a while, as a waitress again.

And so we went. Six weeks of hard-core backpacking through Thailand, Laos and Vietnam. We didn't travel by private jet during this trip, and we certainly didn't stay in luxurious $800-a-night hotels. But we definitely had an adventure.

We hiked, we motorbiked, we travelled by train to here, there and everywhere. On the trains, we shared cramped sleeping compartments with other people. Jacob would take the bottom bunk; I'd sleep in the top bunk with all our stuff behind me so no one could steal it. We soaked up all the typical experiences of young tourists on a budget: Bangkok's colourful Khaosan Road, filled with its backpacker bars, exotic restaurants and cheap hotels, and Ho Chi Minh City's Cu Chi tunnels, which had once served as everything from communication and supply routes to hospitals and living quarters for North Vietnamese soldiers during the Vietnam War. We enjoyed a slow two-day boat ride from Chiang Khong, Thailand, to Luang Prabang, Laos, cruising past jungles and seeing elephants. I spent so many lazy hours just letting my arm dip into the water as the boat drifted in the hot sun, I ended up with a scalding sunburn on my lower arm, which bothered me for the next two weeks.

In Vang Vieng, Laos, we rented inner tubes and floated down the Nam Song River. Every few feet, it seemed, we encountered yet another bar whose proprietors were hoping to lure us to the shore. Although those bars were usually jammed with partying backpackers, we'd luckily arrived in low season and had the river mostly to ourselves. Once, we pulled over to the side of the river where a family was selling beer from their hut. We played with their goats and chickens and cats, and conversed awkwardly with the family through hand gestures.

In Sapa, high up in Vietnam's Hoang Lien Son mountains near China, we filled two spectacular days just trekking around the region's stunningly beautiful rice field terraces, which were carved like undulating green ribbons into the mountain slopes. At night, we stayed with a local family who made us dinner. I volunteered to help cook and clean. "Oh, you don't have to help us," they told me, but I said, "In my family, if you don't cook, you have to clean." When I tried to wash the chopsticks one by one, however, they just laughed. "No, no, no. You do it like this." And they'd take a bunch of chopsticks in one hand, stick them into the soapy water and wipe them clean. I learned.

Jacob and I visited every temple we encountered. On our first full day in Bangkok, we ended up in the Grand Palace in the middle of a downpour, listening to the rain beat on the roof while people meditated in front of the famous Emerald Buddha, Thailand's most precious religious icon. It was so serene and beautiful to hear the rain, to sit and pray in the silence.

Later, we spent four days at a Buddhist meditation retreat in Koh Samui, an island off the east coast of Thailand. We ate only rice and water. We slept on wooden slabs, with no pillows, no blankets and no hot water for showers. You had to be silent the whole time. No music, no books, no anything. Jacob and I weren't even allowed to speak to one another, sit together for meals or sleep in the same dorm. Each day began at five in the morning, meditating with the monks. You understood that their minds were somewhere yours had never been. They were so still, so at peace and yet so spiritually present. It was an amazing experience, but it pushed me far outside my own comfort zone. Initially, I assumed the silence would be easy for me, since I don't enjoy talking to people I don't know. But it was difficult. You're just so totally in on yourself. When we left and were finally able to talk, I just burst into tears.

"What's wrong?" Jacob wanted to know.

"I don't know," I said. "That was just so hard."

It all was. Despite our exciting adventures, the dark cloud of our unknown future always hovered just above our heads. Neither of us seemed happy with the other. We went to Koh Pha-ngan, another island just north of Koh Samui, and found a great room at a great price during one of the off-weeks between its famous full-moon raves. We'd get up every morning, enjoy a Thai massage and then go explore the island on our rented motorcycle, discovering amazing beaches and eating seafood by the beach—and yet I could see Jacob was depressed.

"We're in the nicest place ever," I said. "How can you be so down?"

"I want to go home."

Another night, just a few nights before we were to return home, we had dinner by the beach on Koh Phi Phi, watched two young kids fire dancing and then wandered back to our hotel room around 10 p.m. with plans to watch a movie. But I fell asleep. When I woke around one in the morning, all the lights were on, the door was open and Jacob was nowhere to be found. I spent two frantic hours wandering all over, checking the bars and the beach. Finally, I saw him stumble out of a bar. I just turned on my heel and walked away. He followed. Finally, I turned on him. "How could you? How could you leave me in the middle of Asia in a hotel on a main road with the door open? We could have been robbed."

Somewhere in the middle of my rant, the night skies opened and the rain poured down on us, silencing any hope for conversation.

The next morning, over breakfast, I tried to explain my anger and my fear. "You didn't even leave a note. We have pencils, paper. You could have written a note: 'Going to have a drink. Be back soon.' But you didn't even bother. I don't understand why you don't understand how that would make me feel."

But he didn't seem to. And that was when I realized he didn't love me anymore.

We returned home to Canada and all the problems we'd tried to leave behind. I quickly landed a short-term HR contract with Dyson, the vacuum cleaner company, but Jacob dragged his feet. He didn't seem interested in trying. "Come on," I'd say. "Move your ass off the couch. Get a job." He didn't. Worse, he became distant again, not answering my phone calls or texting me back. Why not? It wasn't as if he had a job or anything else to do.

On September 14, 2014, I came home from work exhausted and crawled into bed. Jacob was already there.

After a while, he said, "I'm not happy."

"Not happy as in you don't want to be married anymore?" I asked.

"Yeah."

I spent the night on the couch, crying. I still believed we could fix things, but Jacob had decided otherwise. I went home to Nova Scotia for a week, and when I returned, Jacob had moved out.

I remember the feelings I had, standing there in our bedroom, opening the closet and realizing all the clothes that had hung next to mine for seven years were suddenly gone. Abandonment. Loneliness.

Although I soon landed a full-time job with Porter Airlines in their HR department—a job I liked—I struggled. I'd spend my day smiling, playing the part, but after I left work and was on the subway, I would break down in tears. At home at night, I'd have a bottle of wine to drink myself to sleep, then get up the next morning and do it all over again.

My friends worried about me. They suggested that I forget Jacob, go on Tinder—then the most popular dating app on the web—and have fun. I wasn't enthusiastic, but I tried it and even went on a few dates that went nowhere. And then, in early November, I returned to the Tinder site. For something to do. This time, Tinder suggested a man named Gerry. I looked at his brief bio and his photos. I can't remember his bio, and his profile picture didn't impress me. He was blond. I don't date blonds. He was also twenty-six; I was twenty-six. I'd only ever dated older men.

My finger hovered over my phone's screen for a while. Swipe left, and he'd be gone. Swipe right and . . .

"Oh, what the hell," I said to myself. "I'll do it." I swiped right, and we matched.

2

Getting to Know You?

Gerry's first Tinder text message back to me was: "You have really white teeth." Awkward. Later, he told me, "Well, I was trying to be original." Our "match" was not off to an auspicious start. It didn't get better quickly.

We exchanged the usual getting-to-know-you messages and what-do-you-do texts. I was on the bus from my job to the subway one afternoon when he texted that he worked in bitcoin. "What's bitcoin?" I asked, and he sent me a link to a *Financial Post* article—actually, a full-page, sponsored-content advertisement made to look like a news story—entitled "Brave New Digital Currency World."

Gerry, who was described as the "founder of QuadrigaCX Bitcoin Exchange," was the star of the article. "He has been focused on developing the most secure, easiest to use trading platform to simplify the buying and selling of bitcoins for a growing audience," it declared. Gerry claimed his company not only employed the "most advanced security measures in the industry," but that it was also the "first bitcoin platform in Canada to hold a money services business licence from FINTRAC (Financial Transactions and Reports Analysis Centre)," whatever that was. And blah blah blah. None of it answered my question about what bitcoin was— or, for that matter, made all that much sense to me. It seemed mostly designed to impress me. It didn't. I rolled my eyes. *This guy's full of it*, I thought.

At the time, I was juggling my still-new $35,000-a-year job at Porter with side gigs serving at wedding banquets and bartending at Mississauga's Living Arts Centre, trying to get out from under my post-Jacob bills. When we split, I ended up with several thousand dollars' worth of shared expenses left over from our trip. I'd put them on my credit card. At the time, I had assumed we would pay them off together, but then we were no longer together. After we returned, and before he left me, I'd also agreed to front him close to $10,000 for his final year of school. I'd taken most of it from savings I'd been accumulating since I began working at sixteen. I rationalized that it was for our future. But then we didn't have one. And then, of course, our divorce cost me, too.

Gerry asked me to dinner the Saturday night after we matched, which was—surprise—November 8. It turned out he lived just ten minutes' drive from me in a new high-rise condominium complex near Mississauga's Square One, the largest shopping centre in Ontario. We agreed to meet at Canyon Creek, a steak house in the mall. That way, if it didn't work out . . . But then, a few days before our date, I texted him, saying I'd finished work early. He texted back, suggesting we meet for a drink that night at Jack Astor's, a bar-restaurant chain, also in the mall.

I wore a burgundy dress and knee-high boots for the occasion. My first face-to-face impression of Gerry? He was way too skinny for me. He wore dress pants and a long-sleeved baby blue dress shirt that was super tight—not grossly so, it fit him perfectly, but that was because he was so skinny—skinnier even than I was at the time. What else? His blond hair was styled up, and his eyes were so blue, the bluest eyes I'd ever seen.

The bartender took our orders. I ordered Shock Top, a Belgian-style white beer. "I'll have a whisky sour," Gerry said. A whisky sour? Back in Nova Scotia, the men I knew all drank beer.

"You don't like beer?" I asked.

"No," he answered. "There's gluten in beer, and I can't have gluten." And that's how I learned about his Crohn's disease.

We had a couple of drinks and exchanged more small talk

about hopes and dreams. I told him I couldn't imagine ever being with anyone who didn't want to travel. "Oh, I love to travel," he said. He'd already been to many more interesting places than I had and had begun far earlier because his parents, who were much wealthier and much keener travellers than mine, had taken him on family vacations all over Europe and to cool skiing destinations in the United States. For me, travelling was mostly still aspirational.

"I want to go everywhere," I said.

"Me, too," he answered.

After a while, we ran out of first-date talk. He reminded me he lived close by, so he said he'd just walk home.

"I'll drive you," I offered.

When we arrived outside the entrance to his building, he asked, "Would you like to come in?"

"For what?" I asked.

"Anything."

I thought, *Well, what the hell?* At the time, I was still living in the cramped, rundown apartment I'd shared with Jacob. Gerry's spacious two-bedroom condo was new, on the thirty-something floor of a building with huge floor-to-ceiling windows that looked out over the sparkling city at night.

"Wow," I said. "You have such a beautiful view." As I stood

there, Gerry sidled up beside me and kissed me. We ended up kissing for a while on the couch, but it all seemed to be moving too fast. "You know what?" I said finally, pulling away. "Maybe I gave you the wrong idea."

Gerry seemed unperturbed. "No problem," he said. But when I left, he just closed the door behind me without a word. He seemed aloof, uninterested. I figured I'd never hear from him again. But the next day, he texted me: "So I'll see you Saturday for our date."

By mid-December, when I went home to Nova Scotia for the Christmas holidays, I'd stopped going out with a guy from the Living Arts Centre I'd been casually dating, and Gerry and I were officially an item. My mother and all my friends—Aly, Anne, Afton—were supportive, though I heard a few suggestions it might be too soon after Jacob. "Maybe it is too soon," I replied, "but it just feels right. So I'm going to go with it."

I'd already landed a new job, due to start in February, as something called a "senior talent acquisition coordinator" in the HR department at Travelers, a huge American insurance company that was trying to expand its business to Canada. My role would be to serve as the link between recruitment and human resources, coordinating interviews with potential employees and then working with the HR managers to integrate new hires into the company. No more sales! Better, I'd be earning $20,000 more a year for doing less work than at Porter, and I was not only guaranteed four weeks' vacation a year, but was also entitled to "buy" two additional weeks of vacation time each year.

I'd finally be able to travel. And now I would have someone to travel with!

"So, TELL me if you think this is weird."

It was January; Gerry and I had flown to Montreal for the weekend, a last free-flight perk during my final days at Porter. We were sitting in a bar, drinking, nibbling on bar food, still in the getting-to-know-you phase. "I'm thinking of changing my name," I said.

"I don't think that's weird at all," he answered. Gerry already knew that Forgeron was my married name because he'd googled me early on and seen our wedding photos. He understood why I wouldn't want to continue to use the last name of the man I was no longer married to, even though it had become the name I was known by at work and in HR circles in Toronto. When I told him my birth name, Gerry said, "Yeah, I can see why you don't like that, either."

Although I wouldn't legally change my name until after we moved to Halifax in 2016, I'd already confided to my sister, Kim, that I didn't want to continue to be Jennifer Forgeron.

"Well, go back to Griffith," she suggested. When I explained why I wasn't keen on that, either, she had a simple solution: "Then just change your name to one you like better."

What? "You can really do that?"

"Yes, totally! I change people's names all the time," she said. Kim worked at Statistics Canada and helped people navigate the process.

"Isn't that kind of weird?"

"Who cares what other people think?"

While I didn't care what most people thought, I realized with some surprise that I did want Gerry's endorsement, a sign of how important he'd already become in my life—and how quickly. Gerry's support was immediate and unconditional. He seemed like a keeper.

But what would I call myself, if not any of those other names? "I want a name with eight letters," I told Kim.

"What about Robertson?" my sister suggested. My father's middle name was Robert.

"But that's got nine letters," I protested. And yet the more I rolled the name Jennifer Robertson around in my head, the better it sounded. Robertson it would be.

* * *

ON OUR FIRST Valentine's Day, Gerry surprised me with a dozen red roses, a reminder of the kind of declaration of love that had been missing in my life for so long, as well as a sign of what was to come. Gerry always marked special occasions—and even those that were not so special—with roses, always red.

In March, we spent four more days at a lodge in Northern Ontario, sharing stories from our lives before. I told Gerry about my relationship with Jacob. "That sounds like the worst relationship ever," he commiserated. He told me about his own ex-girlfriend, a woman named Christine. They'd met during his first year at the University of Toronto's business school and were together for five years before breaking up the year before. She was a "lovely girl," he told me. "We just wanted different things. She's very attached to her family and not very adventurous." Gerry was looking for someone independent and strong, which, he suggested, was where I came in.

The reality was that Gerry was still finding his own feet again after what had seemed like a lost year. Besides his breakup with Christine, he'd been diagnosed with Crohn's and had almost died before doctors realized what was wrong. The condition was now under control with medication, he said. He'd also recently moved to Toronto from Vancouver and had started a new business he was very excited about.

That new business was Quadriga Coin Exchange, also known as QuadrigaCX, a bitcoin exchange Gerry and his business partner, an older man named Michael Patryn, had incorporated in British Columbia almost exactly a year before we met on Tinder. "It's where you buy and sell cryptocurrency," Gerry explained to me, describing it as being "like magic beans on the internet that you can sell for real money." It definitely did seem to me as fanciful as that fairy tale, "Jack and the Beanstalk."

Why Quadriga? In Greek mythology, a quadriga—a chariot drawn by four horses abreast—is known as the "chariot of the gods." Gerry knew that, but he told me he'd chosen it mostly because it sounded good and worked well as a website address.

I eventually learned that bitcoin—a form of crypto-, or secret, currency that does not exist as paper or coin, but only in digital form, and can be bought and sold and valued in transactions that are beyond the control of banks or governments—was "invented" in 2009 by a mysterious and perhaps not even real person (or maybe people) operating under the name Satoshi Nakamoto. Nakamoto had published a paper on a cryptography mailing list at the height of the global financial crisis, outlining a system using complicated cryptography to make sure no one could spend the same digital currency twice, thus finally making it both secret and secure. He/she/they/it even helpfully included open-source code, so others could transform the theoretical currency into electronic-cash-system reality.

The first commercial bitcoin transaction took place in 2010, when a computer programmer in Florida bought two Papa John's pizzas for 10,000 bitcoins. By July 2010, the real-world value of a single bitcoin had rocketed from eight 10,000ths of a dollar to . . . well, eight cents. But its value continued to increase erratically, if exponentially, as bitcoin began to be discovered by all manner of investors, from curious financial dabblers to anti-government, anti-bank, anti-establishment activists and even criminals who found the Byzantine world of bitcoins to be an irresistible, as well as convenient, means to mask their black market transactions. The value of a bitcoin fluctuated wildly. Consider 2013, for example, the year Gerry began Quadriga. At the beginning of that year, you could buy a single bitcoin for $13.50. In early April, the same bitcoin was worth $220. A few weeks later, it had tumbled back to $70. On December 4, the price peaked for the year at $1,079 per magic-bean bitcoin before dropping three days later to $760, a collapse of nearly thirty percent. Still, the ever-upward long-term trend seemed clear.

I didn't know any of this at the time. What I did know was what Gerry told me, which was that he'd begun buying and selling bitcoin when it was "dirt cheap" and had made a "lot of money" as a result. At this point, he was doing well financially, but he was far from the rich man he would become. He had a nice apartment, but nothing out of the ordinary for an up-and-coming young entrepreneur in Toronto. The furnishings were mostly hand-me-downs his mother had given him. He had a business, but no office. He worked out of the apartment, on a laptop. He drove an Audi, but it was a used one. His clothes were ordinary, the kind you could buy off the rack at Walmart or the Bay. He never wore jewellery; he wasn't flashy.

Gerry never told me exactly how much money he'd made, and to be truthful, I never asked. Gerry was a private person. "Everyone has the right to privacy," he would say. But it wasn't just Gerry. I grew up knowing without being told that it was impolite to pry into other people's personal financial affairs, even if that other person was your significant other.

So the truth is, I didn't know all that much about Gerry or his business. What I did know—what mattered to me then—was that this man would not be an anchor, pulling me down, but a life raft, buoying me up. I was happy knowing I had finally met a man who was as eager to make a success of his life as I was of mine.

* * *

WE ALREADY HAD our pet name—the same one—for each other. It was the beginning of April 2015, and we were just hanging out together one day, drinking wine, enjoying each other's company. "Booboo," I began, "I want to live with you."

"Mmmm," he replied. "OK."

It was as simple as that. Except it wasn't. I was still dragging my Jacob debt behind me, and the idea of splitting the monthly rent and utilities on a condo like Gerry's was well beyond my means. I was already juggling three jobs.

"Don't worry," Gerry said. I could move in with him, and he'd continue to foot the bill for all the routine living expenses. He was paying them anyway, so why not? Of course I paid for my personal expenses—my car, insurance, gas, clothing and incidentals—and I continued to chip away at the credit card debt, which meant I still waitressed and bartended on the side.

We had decided we would go on our first big trip together—to Japan, the number one destination on Gerry's bucket list—at the end of April, after which I'd move in with him. But again, the trip would cost money I didn't have and couldn't spare if I was ever to get out from under my own financial obligations. Once again, Gerry offered a simple but generous solution. When he and Christine had gone to Europe, he told me, he'd offered to pay her way if she agreed to plan the trip. "If you plan Japan," he said, "I'll pay for it."

As someone who'd already wandered the globe vicariously by reading other people's adventure blogs, I had plenty of ideas for what we should do, where we should go and how we should get there.

Make no mistake: this vacation wasn't even a close cousin to the opulent adventures we would later share together. We flew economy on the eighteen-hour direct flight from Toronto to Tokyo. I can still see a forlorn-looking Gerry sitting, uncomfortable and sleepless, in the middle seat. We stayed in inexpensive hotels. We rented a car—Gerry had volunteered to drive it, even in an unfamiliar country, and even though he got us lost often—and we spent a glorious week visiting major cities all over mainland Japan, wandering through exotic downtowns, mountains and beaches.

Why Japan? Gerry the Germaphobe's fascination with the country had much to do with what he saw as Japan's sense of order and discipline. Japan was civilized, clean. Public bathrooms—even in gas stations, he marvelled—sparkled from regular cleaning. He—we—were also devotees of Japanese food, especially sushi and yaki, so we happily dined our way through the country.

During the Easter long weekend before we left for Japan, but after we'd decided to live together, Gerry took me to Belleville, Ontario, two hours east of Toronto, to meet his parents, Bruce and

Cheryl, who lived in a large brick house on a quiet street in a comfortably middle-class neighbourhood. They already knew about my existence. Gerry had told his brother, Brad, about me, and he'd told the family. Gerry seemed embarrassed that his love life had become the subject of family gossip and speculation. Someone even found a photo of me, which they'd shown to Gerry's grandmother. "Is she Chinese?" she'd demanded. His grandmother definitely wasn't keen on the possibility of any relative of hers being in a relationship with a foreigner. "No," she was reassured, "she's not Chinese."

The weekend itself went surprisingly well. Brad and his girlfriend, Jess, weren't able to make it, but we had a good time with his parents, wandering around various local antique shops—Bruce and Cheryl owned their own very successful antique store—enjoying dinners together at their home and getting to know one another. I even met his grandmother, who turned out to be friendly.

Gerry's biggest concern that weekend was how to get his mother to give him back the only extra key to his condo without having to answer too many of her questions. When he moved in, he'd given her the spare key, which had been designed so that it couldn't be copied easily, for safekeeping. But now he wanted it for me. "My mom's so nosy," he told me. Though we'd already decided I would move in with him when we returned from Japan, he hadn't told his parents yet and didn't seem keen to open up that discussion.

"Gerry, just tell her it's for me," I said. But he couldn't, or at least wouldn't.

"I just prefer her not to be in my business," he told me.

The result was an awkward dance. "Mom, where's my key?" Gerry asked.

"Why?" she replied.

"Well, I just need a spare key."

"What for?"

"Because . . ."

She eventually gave it to him, but not before reaching her own conclusion. "Oh," she said. "Something's up."

Gerry just laughed. "Yeah, OK." But he didn't explain. I got the sense, which only grew over time, that he didn't tell his parents very much about his life at all.

At the time, I believed he told me everything.

WHAT DID I KNOW about Gerry's life before me—and even, perhaps, his life while we were together? Not as much as I thought I did.

I knew about Christine, of course, and Jeff and Nikki, a couple Gerry and Christine had been friends with and who continued to be Gerry's friends, even after the breakup. We'd go out with them occasionally for drinks or dinner in Toronto. I attended Nikki's birthday party, and we gave them a baby present when we found out they were expecting twins. Other close friends of Gerry's? I can't recall.

I had plenty of friends of my own, even in Toronto. Work colleagues who became friends, people I'd met at social occasions who'd progressed from acquaintances to close friends. I'd always been able to connect with people; Gerry, not so much. The reality—and he would have said this himself—was that Gerry didn't like people, didn't seek them out, didn't want anyone to get too close to him. That was easier because he worked at home and rarely left his condo to socialize. His friends were mostly virtual, and most of them had some connection with business. Even though they were business partners in Quadriga, for example, I never met Michael Patryn face to face, or anyone else connected to the company that was at the centre of Gerry's work life.

Gerry began his workday at seven o'clock each morning and never seemed to stop. When I first moved in with him, the centre of his work life was a tall glass-topped table in the middle of the sparsely furnished living room. Gerry spent hours there, sitting ramrod straight, typing away so fast on his laptop, you could barely hear the keys. His computer was always a Mac. "You should have a Mac for all your computer stuff," he insisted to me.

I tried switching from my PC, but without much success. "Why am I dealing with this Mac?" I'd say. "It's so confusing."

"You can't get viruses," he replied. "People can hack you, but they can't hack you on a Mac." Having my computer hacked had never been among my biggest fears, but it seemed to be so for Gerry. He'd encrypted all his laptop computers—he seemed to have a collection—and refused to store any of his data in the cloud. At the time, I thought of that as nerdy Gerry being super nerdy and didn't give it another thought.

When he wasn't typing—and often while he was—Gerry would be on his cellphone, texting people whose names he rarely mentioned, responding to messages I never saw, conducting business. Ironically, his cellphones—he also had more than one of them—were always Androids. We were again opposites; I loved my iPhone. I kept asking him why, if he was so passionate about Mac computers, he preferred Android phones. But he never gave me a reason, and I never convinced him to change.

I had better luck with his workspace. "How are you actually even comfortable?" I wanted to know as I watched him, perched on a chair in front of the tall table in the living room. I eventually convinced him to buy an IKEA kitchen table, which then became his new "office." The condo's second bedroom, which Gerry had originally intended as his office but never used, became my workspace. I took over its closet, too, but I shared the room with boxes of documents Gerry stored there. I never bothered to look to see what might be in them. Why would I?

What I did bother to consider—and often—was the reality that Gerry, the workaholic bitcoin entrepreneur, was earning far more income and carrying far more of our day-to-day living expenses than I did—or could. I felt guilty. "Should I be doing something more?" I would ask.

"No, don't worry about it," was his inevitable response. "I just want you to be happy. Chill out."

IN JULY, Gerry and I went on our first major cruise together. We flew to Iceland and then on to Denmark, where we boarded a Norwegian Cruise Line vessel for a fourteen-day journey around the Baltic Sea: Finland, Germany, Russia, Estonia, Sweden. The most memorable, and perhaps ultimately telling, moment of the cruise happened on the ship's promenade deck beside the pool one afternoon when Gerry accidentally spilled his Long Island iced tea on his laptop.

Normally, Gerry was just unflappable. If something bad happened, he'd just say, "Not ideal . . . problem for future Gerry." But this time, he was so upset, he was speechless. He threw his hands up in the air in shock and just stared wordlessly at his alcohol-fritzed computer screen. He didn't shout, he didn't swear, but his stunned silence that afternoon actually seemed much worse. Finally, he just exhaled. "Oh my God," he said. Looking at his face, you would have thought someone close to him had died. I'd never seen him so panicked.

The moment didn't last long. He soon remembered he'd encrypted my laptop as well as his own. Gerry encrypted everything. It may sound strange, but Gerry was always paranoid someone would somehow get access to his information. That was just Gerry. So he borrowed my laptop until we arrived in Finland, but as soon as we docked, he went straight to the Apple store and bought a new one.

At the time, I assumed Gerry was simply worried he would lose touch with his business if he didn't have access to his own computer. What was on that computer? I don't know. I do know Gerry said it was fried beyond repair. But Gerry still brought it home with him.

* * *

"CAN I HAVE your credit card number?" We were eating dinner at a restaurant in Square One. Gerry was in a buoyant mood. Quadriga was doing very well. Gerry didn't tell me how well, but I know now that the value of a bitcoin had jumped by fifty percent from the beginning of the year to that evening in the restaurant in August 2015.

As happy as I was for Gerry, it only made me feel sorrier for myself. I was exhausted, still working nine to five, Monday to Friday, at my day job and then racking up at least a few weeknights, plus every weekend evening, waitressing and bartending, standing on my feet late into the night, and still not getting ahead financially. My sadness must have been more apparent than I'd intended. Out of the blue, Gerry asked for my credit card number and then, just like that, paid off all my credit card debt.

More importantly, he told me he had a proposal that he suggested could help both of us.

As his business had grown rapidly, he was struggling to keep up. One of the biggest problems was that he needed to be able to seamlessly transfer money to and from his growing client base. But Quadriga itself wasn't big enough to hire a dedicated professional payment-processing firm to handle those tasks, and that had created a banking bottleneck. The banks, which were skeptical of cryptocurrency to begin with, wouldn't allow him to transfer more than $10,000 a day from his account, and there were only so many banks in Canada anyway. His stopgap solution—until he could afford a processing company—was to hire freelance contractors he trusted. These individuals acted as intermediaries, each of them setting up corporate accounts and then processing funds for his clients up to their individual daily limits. The contractors made money by taking a small percentage of each transaction. With his business growing but not yet big enough, Gerry told me, he needed more freelance contractors. So . . . would I be interested in becoming one of them?

"I know you've been talking about freelancing your HR services," he said. I had. "So why not set up a company to process payments for me?" Soon after, I established Robertson Nova Consulting Inc. and began transferring funds to Quadriga clients.

My role was simple. Gerry would deposit money destined for clients into my corporate account and then send me lists of their names and email addresses and the amount I was to send each of them. I'd either send the funds by wire or e-transfer. I'd get paid in the same way as any other contractor. The amounts per transaction were usually small, a few dollars, but they added up, and over the course of a month, I'd usually earn an extra $1,000, sometimes even more. That not only allowed me to give up my other part-time jobs, but since I could process payments from anywhere at any time, it also meant Gerry and I could more easily indulge our travel dreams.

Should I have asked more questions? Gerry was my boyfriend; I lived with him rent-free in his condo, and he'd paid for our trip to Japan and wiped out my debts. For the first time in my life, I felt financially secure. We weren't rich, but we were better off than I'd ever been. I could buy the expensive cheese at the grocery store, or as many avocados as I wanted. When you know you have money, you're not afraid to look at your bank account or worry about when a bill is due.

So, when Gerry asked for my help with his company—a start-up he was clearly passionate about and was working very hard to turn into a success—why would I say no?

I stopped processing payments soon after we moved to Halifax and bought a house in 2016. By then, Quadriga had become successful enough to hire commercial payment processors to handle client transactions. And Gerry and I had become so intertwined—we'd begun talking about marriage—it seemed odd for him to pay me to work for a company whose success we shared. "Here," I said to him at some point. "Here are the passwords to my accounts. You take over."

The fact is, I knew nothing about Quadriga's clients beyond what I needed to know to send them money. I never interacted with any of them directly, had no access to their accounts or the Quadriga platform, had no say in the company's business decisions and never bought or sold a single bitcoin in all the time I was with Gerry.

I do remember Gerry telling me how careful he was to make sure his clients were legitimate, his business above reproach. He boasted that his business had been the first cryptocurrency exchange in Canada to hold a money services business licence from FINTRAC, the agency that had been mentioned in that first clipping he sent me and which he now explained was Canada's anti–money laundering authority. If the RCMP came to him with concerns about someone Quadriga was dealing with—perhaps an organization the authorities suspected might be using bitcoin to launder drug profits—Gerry told me he was always quick to cooperate fully with them, as long as they produced a warrant. He had to strike a delicate balance, he explained, between protecting his clients' privacy and making sure they were operating within the law. The most important thing, Gerry said, was "KYC: know your client." He assured me he did. So I didn't worry. And never imagined the man I should be worried about was the man who told me not to worry.

3

Our Nova Scotia Home

Celebrating Christmas in Paris. Ballooning over Dubai to mark my birthday. Watching the cherry trees blossom in Washington, DC. Indulging in a road trip through Austria and Switzerland. Toasting the second anniversary of our first Tinder date in Aruba.

As our travels became more frequent, our destinations more exotic, Gerry set up a travel-blogging Instagram account for me and encouraged me to post photos from our adventures using hashtags like #luxurytravel. His idea was that I could use the account as a springboard to a new money-making business—a go-to website for high-end travellers, similar to some of the professional travel blogs I followed on the internet. I tried it for a while. The account was deliberately upbeat, even over the top. Billing myself as a "travel addict and globetrotter," I cheekily captioned one photo of Gerry and me beside the pool at the Hilton Dubai Jumeirah in Dubai: "Sippin' Singapore Slings on my 28th!" But my personal Instagram account, which I only shared with friends, was much more modest, and while it showed many pictures of Gerry and me on our travels, it wasn't boastful or self-indulgent, and there were no #luxurytravel hashtags. After a while, as we began earning so much income from other sources—Gerry from Quadriga, me from a property rental company—the blogging-for-business account no longer made sense, and I gave it up.

Before I met Gerry, the idea of globe-trotting, luxury travel and sipping Singapore slings by a pool at a luxurious resort in Dubai belonged in galaxies distant from my reality. But when this new reality suddenly, unexpectedly, became my own new normal, I was grateful rather than suspicious.

The Gerry I lived—and travelled—with not only seemed like a smart, savvy businessman, but also a generous, thoughtful, eager-to-please boyfriend. He would greet me at the door with a kiss, even if I had just returned from the gym. He left sticky notes around the condo with loving messages for me to find. Gerry not only shared my desire to see the world, but he was also eager to make all my travel dreams come true.

One small example: when Jacob and I backpacked in Southeast

Asia, I'd planned for us to enjoy what I'd read was an amazing hot-air balloon expedition that would let us experience the Laotian countryside from the sky. At the last minute, Jacob backed out. "We can't afford it," he said. Later, after I'd told Gerry how disappointed I'd been, he surprised me with an even more breathtaking hot-air balloon ride over the Sahara Desert for my twenty-eighth birthday. After that, balloon rides became the sort of adventure experience we sought out on our travels.

Although I often asked, especially early on, whether we could afford whatever exciting adventure Gerry had suggested, he always insisted we could. Based on what I knew at the time—and what much of the world understood—there seemed no reason to believe we couldn't.

According to a financial prospectus I read about later, Quadriga claimed to be processing "between sixty and ninety percent of the volume of digital currency exchange transactions in Canada" by November 2015. In 2017, Quadriga would process nearly two billion US dollars' worth of trades from 363,000 individual accounts. Each side of each transaction earned revenue for Gerry. Meanwhile, bitcoins themselves kept increasing in value—from $500 (US) at the beginning of 2016 to almost $800 by the end of the year and then to an unbelievable $13,000 less than a year later.

I didn't know—didn't need to know—those details. All I needed to do in order to believe Gerry was rich beyond what had once been my wildest dreams was to look around our residences, beginning with when we were still in Toronto and the business was still growing more steadily than spectacularly.

Gerry supplied bitcoins to a friend who owned a bitcoin ATM machine at a Toronto co-working space known as Decentral. Customers would feed their cash into the ATM—it didn't take debit cards—and the machine would spit out a certificate showing how many bitcoins the user had purchased. Once a month, Gerry would go downtown—one of his few forays outside the condo—and return home with his cash earnings. Once, when he couldn't go himself, he asked me to pick the money up for him. It wasn't as if I was furtively meeting someone in a dark alley to make a shady deal; I just walked from my Travelers office to Decentral at King and Spadina, got Gerry's cash—he'd called ahead to say I was coming—and then took the GO train back to our condo. But I was terrified. I had multiple thousands of dollars in cash in my bag!

As Gerry explained it to me, he needed the cash to send to Quadriga customers who had chosen the cash-withdrawal option on the company's website. He hadn't been able to convince the banks to handle cash withdrawals for him, so he took care of them himself. He'd stuff cash—actual bills—into prepaid express envelopes and mail them to his customers!

"Could you get some more envelopes?" he'd ask almost every time I went out. At one point later, when we were living in Fall River, Nova Scotia, we bought up our local post office's entire stock of express envelopes. I would bring them to him, but Gerry was always the one who filled them and addressed them to customers. When it got busy, he'd sit there all day, shoving money into envelopes. And then one of us would drop the envelopes off in a mailbox. Gerry ultimately fulfilled $14 million worth of client withdrawal requests using cash.

Gerry continued to deal in cash over all the time we were together, but the piles grew bigger and bigger. "This is $3 million right here," Gerry told me once in the winter of 2018. By then, we were spending the winter in our second house in Kelowna, British Columbia. Gerry had just returned from meeting Adam O'Brien, a successful young entrepreneur who ran a company called Bitcoin Solutions, which operated the first bitcoin ATMs in Alberta and Saskatchewan. Gerry supplied O'Brien with bitcoins, too, so O'Brien would frequently bring Gerry suitcases filled with cash—$20 million in total, I learned later—just from the sale of his bitcoins.

At some point, someone took a photograph of the large

polished-granite island in our Kelowna kitchen. The island was covered with dozens of thick, neatly organized and bundled stacks of $20, $50 and $100 bills. But beyond camera range, there was loose cash everywhere, too, mainly $100 bills, sometimes all over the floor of Gerry's home office, even stuffed in the console of his car. At one point in 2017, Gerry told me the price of a single bitcoin had risen to $25,000 (Canadian), and he was earning $10 million a month.

It was weird at first, I'll admit, but then it began to seem normal. Although Gerry was far more secretive about far more than I knew, he always seemed upfront with me, including about the source of all his cash—that it came from Adam's ATM, or Decentral, or wherever. And, while Gerry and I would marvel at just how surreal it seemed to have so much cash floating around, he would also always make the point: "Too bad it's not ours." And go back to shovelling money into envelopes to send to customers.

I understood from Gerry that cryptocurrency was still new, so old-school, conventional bankers were often suspicious of it. That was one reason why Gerry said he worked so hard to verify the bona fides of his customers. As bitcoins became more popular and more people wanted them, Gerry explained he had begun hiring contract customer-service reps to verify that his customers were who they said they were. But after a while, with so much buying and selling, even his reps couldn't keep up with the demand. Gerry himself was always so busy, so stressed. He'd be working, working, working, day and night. I believed him. I believed in him.

I certainly wasn't the only one. "He was a quiet, serious guy with big plans . . . an honest guy," Adam Goldman, the founder of Bitbuy.ca, another digital currency platform, would later tell CBC News. Frederick Heartline, who'd organized a popular Vancouver bitcoin meet-up group Gerry attended when he lived on the West Coast, described Gerry to a reporter from the *Financial Post* as "super competent and super smart." Amber Scott, an anti–money laundering expert who worked at a compliance firm in Toronto and had been initially skeptical of Quadriga, told *Vanity Fair* she met Gerry at Decentral in Toronto in 2015. According to the article, "She found him funny and sweet. She believed in him. She decided that his involvement might mean that Quadriga was legitimate after all. She appeared with him, and even introduced him, at conferences."

Even before I met him, Gerry was already a well-known and sought-after cryptocurrency advocate. According to a *Bloomberg* profile, he often spoke at financial technology conferences, was a member of the Bitcoin Foundation and served as an advisor for something called the non-profit Crypto Consortium. He was frequently interviewed about the business of bitcoins and even starred in a 2013 online video in which he awkwardly—Gerry was not the most comfortable man around children—helped two preschool kids insert a $100 bill into Canada's first bitcoin ATM in Vancouver to demonstrate just how easy it was to convert ordinary cash into bitcoins.

In November 2013, a year before Gerry and I matched on Tinder, he and Michael Patryn, who would later emerge as a mysterious and perhaps nefarious figure in the Quadriga saga, jointly incorporated Vancouver's Quadriga Coin Exchange to make it easier for Canadians to buy and sell bitcoins. As their business grew, they came up with a plan to take the company public and install bitcoin ATMs across Canada.

I didn't know about any of this at the time. After Gerry and I moved in together, he did tell me he and Patryn were trying to get QuadrigaCX listed on the stock exchange, but he shared none of the details. At one point, Gerry informed me he had to fly to Montreal to meet with Patryn and a potential investor. Another time, in the aftermath of a blowout fight they had, Gerry, who rarely swore, described Patryn to me as a "fucking asshole."

That argument had been about going public. Patryn apparently still wanted to, but Gerry had cooled on the idea after realizing just how much time and energy it would require. After their confrontation, Patryn, his fiancée, Lovie Horner, and a Patryn associate named Anthony Milewski all resigned from QuadrigaCX's board of directors, leaving Gerry as the company's president, sole director and controlling figure. After that, Quadriga operated almost completely inside Gerry's head and his laptop.

Others have confirmed that the company became Gerry. "Looking back," Christine Duhaime told the *Financial Post* in 2019, "I don't know that anybody knew anything about the inside of Quadriga." Duhaime was a Canadian lawyer and a certified financial crime and anti–money laundering specialist. She worked briefly with Gerry in 2015 after he announced plans to create Canada's first blockchain research and development lab. After that plan fell through, she said, they'd drifted apart. She was surprised later to discover he'd moved to Nova Scotia. "I was like: 'Oh, he was in Nova Scotia?'" she told the *Post*. "'I thought he was in Toronto.'"

GERRY AND I BEGAN talking about buying a house together in the fall of 2015. "My company's more stable now, and you have a pretty good job," Gerry said by way of raising the subject. But he was adamant that Toronto's housing market was far too expensive for us to ever consider buying a home anywhere inside the city where we lived and worked and played.

That may seem strange, given Quadriga's spectacular success and continuing growth, as well as what would become Gerry's own notoriously lavish personal spending habits. But Gerry had a complicated relationship with wealth, and he could be almost comically cautious. When we travelled, for example, he would insist we top up the gas in the tank of a rental car before we dropped it off because, he said, the rental company would over-charge to fill it.

In truth, Gerry wasn't the only one with a complicated relationship to our growing wealth. We were, as we liked to joke, the "weirdest rich people" we knew. We never had to ask whether we could afford something, but I still shopped at Walmart. I bought Gerry's clothes; he set a limit of $50 for a shirt. We still enjoyed Happy Meals together from the McDonald's drive-through. We loved that about each other.

So, Toronto was out. "What about Barrie?" Gerry suggested. When I worked at Porter, one of my co-workers had been from Barrie, a bustling, fast-growing city of close to 150,000 people about an hour's drive north of the city. While the cost of living there would be easier to manage, I also remembered my co-worker telling me she lived in an apartment in Toronto during the week, only able to go home to be with her family on weekends. Gerry might be able to operate from anywhere with only his laptop for company, but I was still employed at Travelers, whose head office was in the heart of Toronto's downtown financial district. The idea of long daily commutes in rush-hour traffic—or worse, weekends-only visits with my partner—was a non-starter for me. So we dismissed the possibility of Barrie, as we did most of the other communities ringing Toronto that were affordable but too far from everything.

"I just wish the housing market was better in Toronto," I complained at one point. "I'm sure we could find a nice, big home in Halifax for half a million dollars."

"Then why don't we move to Halifax?" he asked, brushing aside reality.

"Because I don't have a job in Halifax," I replied, logically enough.

"Well," he said, "I have enough put aside already—$200,000— to invest in a house. We could go splits on it. Even if you don't find a great job in Halifax right away, we'll be fine because we'll already have a lot of equity in it."

We decided to take the leap. Luckily, when I told my bosses at Travelers I was moving to Nova Scotia, they quickly offered to let me keep my job and work from their Dartmouth office instead.

In the end, we bought a comfortable but not ostentatious house at the end of Kinross Court, a quiet cul de sac in Fall

River, a fast-growing Halifax suburb. We called it Kinross. Growing up in nearby Bedford, my childhood dream had been to one day live in Fall River, which had always seemed familiar to me, a middle-class community full of nice modern homes. Gerry, who'd spent his childhood in a small-ish Ontario town, was also keen to live close to—but not in—a city and wanted a house with a big yard. We flew to Nova Scotia in early February, stayed with my mother and stepdad and spent two days looking at a number of houses in Fall River I'd found online. After putting in a bid on one, we sat around my mother's house, all of us drinking wine, waiting nervously for the real estate agent to call to tell us if our offer had been accepted.

It had, but there was a problem. I wasn't able to get a mortgage for my half of the $425,000 purchase price. "Not to worry," Gerry said. He came through—as he so often did—with the rest of the money we needed to buy the house. At the time, he told me it represented his entire life savings.

I soon embarked on an ambitious whole-house renovation plan. I was just twenty-eight; I couldn't believe I had a house of my own to decorate and fill with furniture. I never thought a home like this would be within my reach before my forties. We painted every room—the interior had been all dark colours—and added a large two-level deck on the back, overlooking Gerry's big backyard and what became the new $100,000 pool with water-falls, a hot tub and pool house. We finished the basement, adding a large open recreation area and a separate exercise room, complete with a sign painted on the wall: YOU DON'T GET WHAT YOU WANT. YOU GET WHAT YOU WORK FOR! At the time, I thought it was a perfect encapsulation of who Gerry and I were: two overachievers whose hard work was paying off.

One thing we didn't need to replace was the soaker tub; its presence had been a major selling point for Gerry. He loved taking baths. Even if we were in a rush to go somewhere, Gerry would often say, "I'm just going to take a quick bath." And he would. He even worked in the bath, bringing his laptop with him. "If people knew you were processing their bitcoins while you're taking a bath . . . ," I'd joke.

Perhaps surprisingly, we had no outside security system. Gerry didn't believe in them. "By the time a security company arrives," he'd said, "everything would be gone." Although Gerry kept a small safe in his office, he depended mostly on his own technology for security. He set up motion-detecting cameras everywhere, monitoring the front and back entrance doors, inside the kitchen, even the pool house. He did the same when we bought our second house, in Kelowna. Once, when we were at Kinross, he told me, "Someone's at our front door in Kelowna." When he opened the app on his phone, however, we discovered it was just two deer hanging out by the door. Gerry was always on his phone, checking his cameras.

He also had cameras installed inside each of his offices, which were located in bedrooms on the second floor of each of our houses. The cameras faced the doors, so he'd always know if anyone came in. Whenever we went away, or if anyone visited, he would lock the office door. I never went into his office unless Gerry was there. On the one hand, I just accepted that as part of Gerry's quirky obsession with privacy; on the other, I had no need to be there alone. It was Gerry's "man cave," minus the TV.

Although he was a sponge for knowledge about every kind of world affair, spending hours when he wasn't doing Quadriga business reading articles on the web, analyzing what was going on in society and talking with me about what it meant, he simply couldn't sit still long enough to enjoy television. We would occasionally watch a movie together, but he would get bored quickly and wander back to his office to do whatever it was I didn't know he did there.

WE DIDN'T yet travel first class all the time. In fact, in October 2016, Anne, Aly and I decided to meet in Nashville for a girls' getaway. Aly and Anne are musical; they wanted to experience the world's country music capital. Adele, Chris Stapleton and Florida Georgia Line were all scheduled to play Nashville that weekend. As for me, I just wanted to experience everything everywhere.

When I mentioned the idea to Gerry, he said not to worry, that he had enough points to cover the cost of my flight on Air Canada. On the flight from Toronto to Nashville, however, I ended up in economy, in the worst seat in the world—next to a foul-smelling bathroom and in the middle of a group of loud, half-drunk women.

After landing in Nashville, I texted Gerry: "That was the worst flight of my life."

He texted back in what felt like a scolding: "Yeah, but you got to fly for free."

We'd checked into our Airbnb, one of four bungalows in a row. As we entered, we noticed a couple of men across the street, watching us. We didn't think much of it. We were eager to experience the city.

"Should we take our passports with us?" one of the girls asked.

Gerry and I always kept our passports on our person if there was no safe in the room, so the girls and I did, too. That turned out to be smart. While we were out, we got a call from our Airbnb host. Our place had been broken into—the door kicked in, the bungalow vandalized, our clothes strewn on the floor, makeup bags dumped on the floor, cash taken from my friends' backpacks, my suitcase smashed open so badly I had to replace it, and my laptop, with all my photos and personal information, stolen. For me, the worst was that someone now had access to my photos and personal material. It felt like a violation.

"Don't worry," Gerry said when I called to tell him what had happened. "I encrypted your laptop," he reminded me. "Even the CIA can't get into that."

THE WEEK after I returned from Nashville, Travelers laid off hundreds of employees, including me. I was devastated, especially after the company had so recently agreed to keep me on, even when I told them I was moving to Halifax.

I had only just begun to come to terms with the reality that I was no longer living paycheque to paycheque. Thanks to the combination of my job and the money Gerry paid me to process bitcoin transactions, I now had thousands of dollars sitting in my bank accounts. In Nashville, when we'd been forced to find other accommodations because the original Airbnb was no longer habitable, I'd been able to tell my friends not to worry. I could afford to pay for a hotel room for all of us.

But what now? Halifax definitely wasn't Toronto when it came to jobs in HR. Could I find another one? And then there were our travel plans. Gerry and I were supposed to go to Aruba the next month, and we already had another adventure—Myanmar, the Maldives, Hong Kong, Macau and Singapore—in the works for January. Should we cancel?

When I'm upset—think my breakup with Jacob—I retreat to the couch in the living room with a bottle of wine and feel sorry for myself. Which is what I did at this point. After a while, Gerry came and sat down beside me. He was holding a slip of paper. "I have to tell you something," he said. "I didn't tell you before because I had to make sure it actually happened." He had won close to a million dollars in an online casino!

Gerry and I both liked to gamble. I'm not sure how it began. Before I met Gerry, I'd only been inside a casino two or three times in my life and bet maybe $100 in total. At the time, I couldn't have afforded more. I knew Gerry's parents liked to gamble when they were on vacation, though they mostly just played penny slots. Gerry would up the ante. "Let's go gamble," he'd say with his infectious laugh, and we would. Whenever we travelled, we would visit the casinos—in Las Vegas, Malta, Amsterdam or Macau, which is known as the Asian Vegas. We'd have dinner, gamble a bit, walk around the city, gamble a bit more, have a few more drinks and then call it a night. It was fun, more fun because we could afford to lose. Not that we ever lost much. We would win some, lose some, mostly coming out even, at worst only down a few hundred dollars at the end of an evening. I didn't worry because cautious Gerry would always set betting limits and stick to them. Still, I hadn't realized he was gambling bitcoins online.

Now he showed me a deposit slip. It was for more than $900,000 (Canadian) and it indicated the money had come from an online casino. At first, we both reacted exactly the way you see on TV. We were jumping around, hugging each other, cheering. But then, after a while, I remembered I still didn't have a job. This windfall was wonderful, but it was Gerry's, still Gerry's money. We might have been a couple, we might have a house together and we might have been planning to spend the rest of our lives together, but I would never feel secure if I didn't have my own job, my own source of income, my own safety net. It was, I'm sure, one more psychological hangover from my breakup with Jacob.

"This is great, and I'm very happy for you," I told Gerry, "but I still need a job."

It was as if Gerry had been expecting that. Why didn't I take our windfall and invest in real estate? he suggested. I could set up my own company, buy properties, rent them and manage them.

"But I'd feel badly taking your money," I replied.

"But it's for us," he insisted. "I'll give you the capital and you build the company, build it for us. If bitcoin dies tomorrow"—Gerry would often say that, for no reason that made sense to me at the time—"then we'll have another source of income that you've created because I don't have the time to build a rental company. You do it."

I thought about it. Gerry had won the million dollars at a casino; it hadn't come from his day job at Quadriga. It was found money. And he was willing to put it up as capital to allow me to start a business. I would have to do the work to build it. For me, for us. Even before Gerry incorporated Robertson Nova Property Management in January 2017, I'd acquired my first rental property, in the north end of Halifax.

Looking back, it's possible to discern a pattern in Gerry's generosity, his eagerness to please and the secretive, manipulative ways in which he went about pleasing. Whenever things didn't seem to be working out for me—when I couldn't afford to move into the condo with him, when I was juggling part-time jobs to stay afloat, when I couldn't get a mortgage, when I lost my job—Gerry would magically swoop in and save the day.

I didn't see that then. What I did see was a challenge—turning the dream of a successful property management company into reality—and I was eager to take it on.

* * *

NOW WHAT? It was November 2016, and I found myself seated alone at a table in the Ruth's Chris Steak House near Palm Beach on the Caribbean island of Aruba, staring into a chilled seafood tower—a mountain-high platter of "Maine lobster, Alaskan king crab legs and knuckles, fresh colossal lump crab meat and jumbo cocktail shrimp"—much more than I could ever consume on my own. Gerry had ordered it for us, but after it arrived, he declared he was too drunk to eat and afraid he was going to be sick, so he decamped to our hotel room. Leaving me alone with the seafood tower.

We had flown to Aruba to celebrate the second anniversary of our first Tinder date. It had been a remarkable two years of love and laughter. We told each other we were the other's best friend. And we were. But Gerry's attitudes, especially when it came to money, could still confuse and confound me in ways I never quite understood. "Why don't we stop at the hotel bar?" I'd suggested when we were about to begin our evening a few hours earlier. "We can get a drink there and then go to the casino."

"But if we go straight to the casino," Gerry answered, "we can get our drinks for free."

"Gerry," I retorted, "that is just so weird." He had already begun to spend huge amounts on expensive possessions he rarely used with barely a nod to how much anything cost. But he could still play bargain hunter when it came to spending a few dollars on drinks. Whenever I'd call him out on these contradictions, he'd just shrug and mumble an excuse. Just Gerry being Gerry.

That night in the casino, he'd gotten drunk on the free drinks. At one point, I went to the washroom, and when I returned, I couldn't find him anywhere. I was beginning to worry when I heard the sirens and saw the flashing lights in the casino's high-roller section. Gerry, drunk, sat at the table, a huge, happy smile on his face. "I just sat down and spun once," he marvelled.

Lucky bugger, I thought. I'd just lost my job, and Gerry, who'd already won a million the month before, had scooped up thousands more tonight. Some people are always lucky.

At the restaurant, Gerry decided we should celebrate. He ordered everything, including the seafood tower. And then he left, too drunk to eat. I picked at the food, tried to eat what I could to justify what he'd ordered, but it was too much. I soon signed for the bill—it was over $400—and went back to our room. I told him how much the bill was and how much food had gone to waste. "But you had to get your free drinks in the casino," I complained. Gerry didn't say anything, just smiled his big, goofy smile. He had the best smile.

* * *

WE DECIDED TO invite Gerry's parents, his brother and his fiancée to Nova Scotia to celebrate our first Christmas in our first house.

It didn't go well—and hadn't even before that. The first thing Gerry's mother, Cheryl, had said after she learned we were moving to Fall River was "Oh my God, you guys are going to live in the boonies!" Really? Gerry's parents lived in Belleville, two hours from Toronto in a community where not much happens; Fall River is just ten minutes from an international airport and half an hour from Halifax. Cheryl also asked, "Who's paying for the house?" At Christmas, her first question was "How did you ever get Gerry to move here?"

I'd spent two weeks decorating the house for Christmas, trying to make everything perfect for Gerry's parents. Then Cheryl breezed in, declared the Christmas tree "ugly, like something you'd see in a department store" and vowed to fix it. Her idea of fixing it was to string candy canes around the tree. I hated candy cane decorations—which I'd already told Gerry the week before, when he'd tried to do the same thing. Perhaps candy canes were a Cotten tradition. The fact that Gerry, who never wanted to confront his mother, then failed to stand up for me in the great candy cane war precipitated one of our few, but most serious, fights.

And Cheryl still wasn't done. "Why are there no handmade ornaments on the tree?" she demanded. Because I'm not a fan, I told her. It didn't matter. On Christmas morning, she presented me with a gift she'd gone out specially to buy for me: an ugly handmade ornament. She also presented me with a trash can for the bathroom. "Why do I need this more than Gerry?" I asked, by this point just to be difficult.

You won't be surprised to know I was relieved when his family left to go home to Ontario and Gerry and I had our house, and our lives, to ourselves once more.

4

Because We Could

No one—certainly not Gerry—doubted he was destined for a far richer and more successful life than the comfortable middle-class existence he'd grown up amidst in Belleville. There's a family story that, when Gerry was just seven, his parents took him and his brother on a first—and only—camping trip. Gerry refused to sleep in a tent on the ground with the rest of the family. He spent the night in the family's van instead, crying to go home to a real bed. Gerry always preferred his comforts.

As someone who'd camped, backpacked and slept in beds that were far from comfortable in places that were well short of luxurious, I'd arrived at our relationship with a very different perspective on life. Still, it was impossible not to bask in the many and various blessings Gerry's bitcoin business had bestowed on us. We weren't yet thirty and we were rich enough to buy the best of everything, travel wherever we wanted, all perks included. Every day, I woke up grateful and in awe. "Oh my God, I can't believe this is my life," I'd say to Gerry. "Life is so amazing." But then I'd quickly switch gears, my own anxieties bubbling to the surface. "What if something bad happens and ruins it all?"

"Yeah," Gerry would laugh, "that's never going to happen."

After a while, I believed him.

Over the course of eighteen months, beginning around the time we moved to Nova Scotia in June 2016 and ending aboard a cruise ship on the Pacific Ocean off the Galapagos Islands in early 2018, our universe unfolded in wonderful ways I could never have imagined or even hoped for.

Thanks to Quadriga, we had seemingly been transformed— super Cinderella-like—from ordinary well-to-do, even wealthy, twentysomethings into a couple on wealth steroids with access to so much money, we couldn't figure out what to do with it all. Sometimes, we bought stuff just *because we could*. We travelled wherever we wanted in a style to which we soon became accustomed *because we could*.

I first realized just how much our lives had changed around the time I planned our first exotic vacation—a six-week adventure in January 2017 to Myanmar, the Maldives, Hong Kong,

Macau and Singapore to celebrate my twenty-ninth birthday. By then, we always flew first class. I realize that may sound boastful and self-indulgent, and perhaps it is. But the truth is, our lifestyle was still all so new to me, I can't help but marvel, even now, at the thought of us snuggling into our pods before takeoff. Gerry would work; I would read. "Bye, Gerry," I would say. "See you in . . . wherever."

Gerry wanted to visit Hong Kong; I was keen to see the Maldives, the tiny chain of islands in the Arabian Sea that was threatened by rising sea levels. Gerry joked that we should see them before they sank. But why not visit both? And why not other countries at the same time? When you have the money, a passion for travel and the freedom to be away for weeks at a time, it all becomes seductive—and addictive. Who would not want to have those opportunities?

At one point during that trip, we ended up at a ferry terminal in Hong Kong, waiting to board a boat for the one-hour trip to Macau. It was a crazy, chaotic scene with long queues and so many impatient people everywhere, you couldn't move. A fist fight broke out between a ship's officer and someone in the crowd. Finally, Gerry saw a sign advertising a helicopter shuttle to our destination. It would cost $700—versus $25 for the ferry—but we'd be there in fifteen minutes. No hassle, no crowds. Gerry looked at me. I looked at him. We could afford it, he said. Why not? I waited while Gerry went to buy the tickets. But he returned a few minutes later without them. In his strange, quirky, Gerry way, the man who'd bought a half-million-dollar yacht because he could had suddenly decided a $700 helicopter ride was too great an extravagance. We took the ferry, where the chaos continued on board; we had to push our way ashore on our arrival. Gerry turned to me. "Next time, the helicopter," he said.

After reading a luxury travel blog called *Bruised Passports*—one of the inspirations for my own short-lived foray into travel blogging—I'd decided we should include a cruise along Myanmar's Irrawaddy River in our vacation itinerary. The blog wasn't just about travel, wrote the couple who had turned their own passion for adventure—ninety-five countries in twelve years—into a full-time travel-writing business. "It's about love and looking at the world through rose-tinted glasses." I liked that approach.

Myanmar, formerly known as Burma, had only recently opened up to tourists after decades of military rule in the midst of one of the world's longest-lasting civil wars. *Bruised Passports* recommended we take the four-night river cruise offered by Strand Cruises, which meandered up the river from Bagan to Mandalay, past royal cities, temples, monasteries and cultural treasures.

From the outside, Strand Cruises appeared to be just one of

many operators hoping to cement their place in the country's fledgling tourism industry. But to call the *Strand* a cruise ship would be misleading. Forget all those great, hulking vessels steaming overnight from one port to the next in the Mediterranean or the Caribbean, each filled to overflowing with thousands of passengers all jammed in together. The *Strand* was a small—just twenty-seven cabins—purpose-built vessel constructed for the owners of the legendary Strand Hotel in Yangon (Rangoon). Each of its spacious cabins featured floor-to-ceiling windows with spectacular views of the river, French balconies, exotic teak-wood flooring and furnishings, luxurious mattresses with down-filled pillow tops, high-thread-count Vietnamese sheets, ensuite baths with marble vanities and plenty of wardrobe space (for me) and satellite Wi-Fi (for Gerry).

Could we afford it? I didn't even have to ask. We upgraded to one of the two end-of-vessel suites with a wraparound balcony and our own separate lounging area. There were actually only three other couples on the ship for our cruise, so the reputed superb service was beyond impeccable. You'd mention you might like a drink, and it would appear in front of you. Once, Gerry decided he'd take his drink back to our room. The Burmese waiter, dressed in a traditional costume, was having none of it. He scooped up Gerry's Long Island iced tea, put it on a tray and insisted on following Gerry back to the cabin with his lone drink perched on the tray. Despite the fact that Gerry usually wanted the best of everything, he hated being fawned over in that public way. "It makes me uncomfortable," he said. Gerry being Gerry.

LOOKING BACK NOW, our lifestyle makeover probably began soon after we moved to Nova Scotia and Gerry began to acquire his dazzling collection of toys—because he could.

It started with a $100,000 Tesla electric vehicle he had to order from California. He loved to take the car on the highway, eat ice cream or popcorn and just let the car drive itself. "Look, Ma, no hands!" he'd yell, delighted with himself. That car became his favourite acquisition. But it was far from his only indulgence.

One day, we were out for a walk with the dogs when Jill Hann, our realtor, texted me a picture of herself and another person standing in front of a small airplane. "Guess where I am?" she asked.

I had no idea. "Where?"

"Gerry's plane!"

Gerry's *what*? I still had no clue what she was talking about. "What's this all about?" I asked Gerry.

"Oh, man!" Gerry tried to make a joke of it. "Only in Nova

Scotia. You can't keep a secret here because everybody knows everybody."

It turned out that Jill had been at a small airport near Truro to get some photos and ended up talking to someone she knew there who pointed out a new private plane on the tarmac. "Half a million bucks," the person marvelled. "Owned by some young guy who does something called bitcoin."

"Gerry Cotten?" Jill asked.

"Yes, that's the guy."

"I'm their realtor," she exclaimed. "I sold them their house." And that was how I found out Gerry had bought a new Cessna 400 turboprop aircraft—without thinking to mention it to me.

"Oh, I was going to tell you," he insisted. "I was planning to surprise you and take you out for a flight one day, but I'm still learning how to fly it."

Was he going to sweep into our house one afternoon and whisk me away for a ride in his plane? I don't know. Looking back, Gerry seemed to be more about secrets than surprises. Whenever I'd suggest we take the plane out for a spin, in fact, he responded with an excuse. "Oh, I'm too busy . . . I haven't learned to fly in clouds yet." He did take me with him once—it was an awesome experience, flying low over the countryside in his small two-seater plane—but it only happened that one time. In the end, I don't believe Gerry flew his plane very often himself, except to train with his flight instructor.

Why did Gerry care so much about acquiring all the trappings of wealth if they never gave him pleasure once they were his? I can't help but think of the scene in that 1990 movie *Pretty Woman* in which Julia Roberts and Richard Gere are in Gere's penthouse. Roberts stands at the balcony, admiring the view of the ocean. When Gere tells her he never goes out there because he's afraid of heights, Roberts is incredulous. Why did he want a penthouse apartment, then?

"It's the best," he answers. That was Gerry.

I WAS SLIGHTLY more involved in another purchase: the *Gulliver*, our yacht.

Gerry and I often talked about how he hoped to pull back from the day-to-day craziness of Quadriga at some point. We would find a boat, take our dogs and sail south, meandering among the Caribbean islands for as long as we wished. It was a crazy dream—neither of us had ever sailed before—but given the world in which we suddenly found ourselves, the one in which dreams do come true, it was easy to believe anything was possible.

During the fall of 2016, Gerry discovered Jeanneau, the famous

French boat designer and builder, in the same way he found most things: online on his laptop. He showed me plans and possibilities.

"Do you like it?" he asked. What was not to like? It was sleek and beautiful and boasted every luxurious appointment any land-lubbing would-be sailor could ask for. We picked and chose from among the many options, settling on an oak-panelled, pink-and-cream master bedroom with two VIP guest bedrooms, two bathrooms, a dining area for six and a full kitchen with a gas stove, dishwasher, washer and dryer. The drop-down swim platform at the stern came standard.

For Gerry, however, the boat's most important qualification was that it be deemed a "yacht." He didn't want just a sailboat. He'd already checked, and he informed me that a yacht was a vessel more than fifty feet long. The Jeanneau we ordered was the fifty-one-foot model. Gerry's other important requirement was that he be able to sail it without a crew—once he learned how to sail—so we could travel on it alone together.

Our new boat—which was built in France, shipped to the United States and driven to Nova Scotia on a big flatbed truck—cost more than $500,000, plus taxes and transportation. Gerry claimed the total made him nervous, but he nonetheless paid cash. While we waited for it to arrive, Gerry discovered a Facebook group about yachts, and we watched, giddy with delight, as people began posting sightings: "A fifty-one-foot Jeanneau is being transferred to Nova Scotia."

"Oh my God, it's our boat," we'd laugh.

The *Gulliver* ended up at Sunnybrook Yachts, a brokerage in Chester, a well-to-do town on the province's South Shore where Gerry learned to sail with one of Sunnybrook's salesmen. Gerry liked him well enough; they spent hours together on the boat. Later, the salesman told *Vanity Fair* he was struck by Gerry's constant smile. "It was a gentle, unflappable smile," the magazine wrote. "It put strangers at ease; it made him seem lighthearted." I was less enamoured of the salesman; I'd stopped attending lessons because I found him condescending to me as a woman. So I wasn't surprised when I also read in *Vanity Fair* that he had described us as a couple "you'd less likely see at Scaramouche than in a Walmart parking lot."

"SO," GERRY said to his mother, "guess which one is ours?"

It was the summer of 2018, and Gerry's parents had returned to Nova Scotia for another visit. One morning, Gerry suggested we drive to the picturesque South Shore for a picnic. When we arrived at the Shining Waters marina, in a sheltered cove near the head of St. Margarets Bay, Gerry pointed to a small dinghy.

"We'll just take that over to the picnic spot," he said vaguely. As we motored away from the dock into a bay filled with dozens of expensive boats bobbing at anchor, Cheryl gave Gerry a look, as if to ask, "What's really going on here?" Gerry was enjoying himself. "Which one?" he asked again, taking in the fleet of big and small sail and motorboats before us.

Gerry's mom didn't miss a beat. "It's the biggest one—that one over there," she declared, pointing to the *Gulliver*. "Yours has to be the biggest and the nicest one in the whole marina."

Gerry laughed. She was right. She knew her son. When he was still in high school, his brother Brad's then girlfriend, Jess, asked Gerry what he planned to be when he grew up. "A millionaire," he answered automatically.

"How are you going to do that?" she wanted to know.

"If I tell you," Gerry fired back with a smile, "I'll have to kill you." It had seemed funny when Jess first told me that story.

The day we took Gerry's parents on their first sail aboard the *Gulliver*, Gerry had yet another surprise for them—or, to be more accurate, revealed one more secret he'd kept from them. As we sailed along the shore near the famous Oak Island, the place where Captain Kidd is supposed to have buried his treasure, Gerry pointed to another smaller island.

"That's our island," Gerry announced.

I'd found Little Island—that was its actual name—on a real estate website. We bought it for $161,000 from Tucker Carlson, the Fox News TV host. It was just two and a half acres, but the idea that we could buy a whole island for ourselves seemed amazing. We agreed we would build a "cottage" there and then sail to it in the *Gulliver*. I'd previously fallen in love with a luxurious dream cottage featured in a local hospital lottery, so we decided we would build an exact replica of it—a 2,500-square-foot, two-storey, three-bedroom, three-bath house—on our new island.

The last time I ventured there, it was a cold day in the fall of 2018, shortly before Gerry and I left for India. The builder and I took a dinghy to the island to inspect the state of construction. The new dock had already been built, and a rough road led up to the house, which had been fully framed in and made roof tight for winter. In the spring, the builder told me, he'd complete the "cosmetics"—installing all the drywall, cabinets, tiles and accoutrements that would make the house our home. I could imagine it all. I didn't have to imagine the commanding views of the bay and the other nearby islands, however; they were visible from the windows of the under-construction master bedroom. We had chosen our location well. The contractor promised the house would be ready for us to move in by the summer of 2019.

Owning land he could call his own had become a big deal to

Gerry. "I've got to have my own land," he would say, then joke, "I'm going to call it Gerryland and then I can make all the rules and regulations." I discovered some waterfront property for sale on Kinsac Lake near Kinross, our house in Fall River. Gerry had already fallen in love with the community, said it felt like home, so I suggested he look at the lakefront land. In the winter of 2017, Gerry and the realtor hiked in to inspect the land on snowshoes. There were actually two properties totalling eight acres, and Gerry decided we should buy both and develop them together. He had grand plans. We would build our "forever house" there. This house, he declared, would have an *indoor* swimming pool and its own helicopter pad. A helicopter pad! We were laughing, almost giddy, not because we actually intended to build a helicopter pad, but because we could. "We can do this!" we said to one another. "Is this real life?"

In May 2017, we bought yet another house for ourselves, this time in Kelowna, British Columbia, a small city of 150,000 in the Okanagan Valley, four hours east of Vancouver. Why Kelowna, which was, after all, 5,500 kilometres west of the place we called home? Well, before we met, Gerry had lived briefly in British Columbia and liked it there. Then, soon after we'd moved in together in Toronto, he travelled to Kelowna for a meeting at a local winery with potential Quadriga investors. I hadn't been able to accompany him on that trip, so Gerry brought me back a gift of wine cherry chocolates. We got to talking, and I told him the story of my own visit to Kelowna when I was in my early teens. A girl I'd grown up with had moved to British Columbia and invited me to visit her family there. I spent a few days with them that summer at a resort in the mountains near Kelowna, overlooking Okanagan Lake. I thought it was the prettiest place I had ever seen, and I told my teenaged self—and later, Gerry—that I would live there someday. Gerry, as was so often his wont, decided to make that dream come true, too.

But there was more to it. While Gerry loved Kinross, it was just comfortably middle-class, and he already had aspirations for something grander. We flew to Kelowna, rented a car and spent a day checking out Kelowna's million-dollar-plus homes before finally deciding to put in a $1.2 million bid on a spectacular five-bedroom, three-bath executive house on Lamont Lane in the upscale Upper Mission District. With its vaulted twenty-one-foot-ceilinged grand entranceway, triple garage, covered deck with private backyard waterfall feature, huge open kitchen and dining area with high-end appliances and oversized granite island, main-floor office with its own entrance—not to mention a loft master bedroom with twelve-foot ceilings, its own cozy gas fireplace and a private deck with sweeping views of downtown

Kelowna and Okanagan Lake, it definitely fit Gerry's need for something grander.

"Are you hungry?" the real estate agent asked after we'd bid. "Why don't we have dinner? My treat. Any preferences?"

McDonald's, we replied. *McDonald's!* She looked at us as if we had ten heads, but she quickly recovered, offering to meet us at a nearby location. We didn't have the heart to tell her we'd prefer the drive-through. So the three of us sat in the restaurant, awkwardly eating our Happy Meals—Gerry's without the bun because of his gluten intolerance—and waited to find out if we'd be allowed to spend more than a million dollars on a house we didn't need.

Our bid was accepted.

OUR DECISION to buy the house in Kelowna led to another decision: to lease a private jet. We'd already been considering the idea; we wanted to be able to bring our dogs, Nitro and Gully (another chihuahua we'd acquired as company for Nitro), on our increasingly frequent travels. If we decided to spend part of the year in Kelowna, we'd definitely want them with us there, too.

Gerry burrowed into all the pluses and minuses of owning our own plane versus leasing it. "If we own it," he explained, "we'd be responsible for everything—the employees, the maintenance, everything. But if we lease, we won't have to worry about anything. We just pay so much a year and we'd get to fly whenever we want to with just a few hours' notice." It was clear Gerry had already made up his mind which option made the most sense to him.

We leased—they called it fractional ownership—a six-passenger Cessna Citation CJ2+ from a Toronto-based company called AirSprint, using our air hours mostly to fly back and forth to Kelowna, but also occasionally to the Caribbean with our friends. Once, we flew my mom and stepdad to Iceland for a vacation. And the jet would come in handy again when we travelled from Halifax to Scotland for our wedding. But that came later.

Having access to your own private jet is an incredible luxury. You bypass all the usual check-in routines and airport security. There would usually be a red carpet on the tarmac to greet you, an attendant to serve you drinks and refreshments, and no one to hassle you about how much luggage you brought. Most of the time, when we landed in a foreign country, we didn't even have to go through a customs inspection. Gerry himself rarely travelled with much more than his laptop bag. For Gerry, I believe leasing his own jet was just another way to say to the world, "Hey, I'm a millionaire and I can afford this."

But wait a minute, you may be asking yourself. Didn't Gerry

already own his own plane? Well, yes he did, but like many of the toys he acquired, the plane didn't live up to Gerry's imaginings, or his expectations. For starters, the single-engine turboprop plane couldn't fly nearly as far or as fast as we wanted to travel. More importantly, no one but Gerry could fly his plane. He couldn't work on his laptop and fly the plane at the same time. And at that point, he was far too consumed with Quadriga to carve out time for flying.

The same was true of the *Gulliver*. Gerry might have dreamed of a life of leisure on the ocean, but the reality was that he was tethered to his laptop and his increasingly demanding business. Managing a fifty-one-foot yacht by himself as a novice sailor turned out to be far more stressful than he imagined when he originally declared he wanted a boat he could sail by himself. In the end, we didn't sail far or often. Once, we took some friends to Peggys Cove, near the famous lighthouse, jumped off and went for a swim. Sometimes, Gerry and I would sail along the coast for the day, then return to the marina in Chester, make dinner, enjoy a few quiet drinks and stay overnight on the boat. But Gerry was always too busy to completely relax.

I DIDN'T KNOW exactly what Gerry was busy doing; I assumed he was so busy because Quadriga was growing so quickly, with more and more investors discovering bitcoin, and he had to stay on top of all that growth. That was true, at least in part. In 2016, Quadriga handled about $72 million in trades. In 2017, the trading volume topped $1.2 billion.

According to a later report by the Ontario Securities Commission, Gerry "presided over a team of contractors, all of whom worked remotely on tasks that included maintaining the technical aspects of the platform, verifying account IDs and responding to customer inquiries," but Gerry was Quadriga's sole gatekeeper. "Everything had to go through him," as one contractor explained. That meant there was no internal oversight, either, let alone the keeping and maintaining of financial records to satisfy basic corporate expectations. Although Gerry assured clients "all funds in the [Quadriga] system are highly liquid, and can be withdrawn at any time," the reality was that clients had no way of verifying those claims beyond taking Gerry at his word. They did. And so did I.

We continued to travel: a quick getaway for some Florida sun over Easter in 2017; extended adventures in Greece, Italy and Malta the next month to celebrate Gerry's twenty-ninth birthday; a few days in Las Vegas in September, gambling with Gerry's parents; Morocco in October . . .

And we continued to buy: the house in BC, the island off Nova

Scotia, the part ownership in the jet. In the middle of all of that, I would learn later, Gerry lost access to $10 million worth of Quadriga cryptocurrency as the result of a "coding error." He never mentioned a word about it to me. I am struck by how well he was able to wall off the various parts of his life from each other, and from me.

When Gerry did mention problems in his business to me, he was always vague. I knew he was frustrated with conventional banks, which he considered "anti-bitcoin." He vented occasionally about finding some way to take Quadriga out of the banking system entirely, but my understanding was that Gerry spoke as a legitimately aggrieved party, an ahead-of-his-time cryptocurrency entrepreneur whose business was being unfairly hamstrung by risk-averse bankers who wanted to control the bitcoin industry.

I keep circling back now, asking myself what I knew and didn't know and why I didn't know what I didn't know. Gerry and I had mutually agreed we would give each other the space to live our own lives within our committed couple relationship. We had talked about that. "I hate someone suffocating me," Gerry would say. "I hate it when someone is always texting me, asking where I am and when I'll be home." We never did.

We were both, it is fair to say, self-focused.

Having lost my Travelers job—and having been embarrassed

and ashamed when it happened—I was desperate to rebuild my own career, my own self-esteem. Then Gerry told me he'd won all that money in a bitcoin casino and offered me a path to redemption. While the capital for my business came from Gerry, I was less concerned with the provenance of the money at the time than I was consumed with putting it to work to build Robertson Nova, my new property management company, so I could contribute my fair share for our mutual benefit.

Gerry encouraged that. "If bitcoin disappears tomorrow . . . ," he would say again, Robertson Nova would keep us going until he found something else.

I worked with a real estate agent to find suitable rental properties. Gerry would recheck the financials to make sure the return on investment seemed viable, and I would then purchase them with cash. At first, that cash came from his casino winnings, but later, as the business grew and I needed more money to buy more real estate, he would deposit what he called his "profits" from Quadriga into my bank account to cover the purchase prices.

In the beginning, I handled everything to do with the business: acquiring, renovating, cleaning, advertising, viewing, leasing, dealing with tenant concerns, even handling evictions. That last was rare; I was a lenient landlord. If the rent was late, a tenant might say, "Oh, I had car problems" or "I lost my job." I'd tell them not to worry. "As long as you communicate with me, we'll work it out." I'd always wanted to create a company I could be proud of, so I was also satisfied to make less money and invest my profits in making the properties nicer. I wanted my tenants to live in the best accommodations. I don't know if Gerry fully agreed with that, but it was my business, so he let me do it. Besides, the truth was, we didn't need the money.

In the beginning, the primary goal of the property management company was to bring in enough income to pay me a decent salary. But then, as the "profits" from Quadriga exploded and it became possible for us to contemplate travelling even more, spending part of the year in Kelowna, even theoretically sailing into the sunset in our yacht, the idea of being tethered to a demanding, hands-on property management company in Halifax became less appealing. We needed someone to take over the day-to-day management while we travelled.

Enter my stepdad, Tom. Although Gerry didn't like very many people, he and Tom got along well. On the surface, they weren't all that similar—Tom was athletic, a hard-core competitive cyclist—but they spent a lot of time together, talking about life in ways Gerry rarely did with anyone else. We knew Tom was unhappy with his job at the post office, so Gerry suggested we ask him to join Robertson Nova as the property manager and look after day-to-day issues while we were away. Gerry had already worked out how much more revenue we'd need to generate each month to justify hiring Tom, so we bought more properties. Eventually, we owned sixteen rental properties worth around $7.5 million.

WE DECIDED to spend from Christmas 2017 until after my birthday in late January 2018 sampling South America, mostly because neither of us liked to be home for Christmas and because neither of us had ever been to that continent. It would become a future-altering event, but not because of anything we actually saw or did on the six-week trip.

We flew to Santiago, Chile, where we boarded a Princess cruise ship, sailed around the tip of Cape Horn, visited the Falkland Islands and made our way to Montevideo, Uruguay, before docking, fourteen days after we departed, in Buenos Aires, Argentina. On New Year's Eve, we gathered in the ship's multi-storey atrium for the midnight balloon drop from its stained-glass dome. Three! Two! One! Gerry and I told each other 2018 was going to be our best year ever, though I could hardly imagine at the time that our life together could become any better than it already was. Or just how awful 2018 would turn out to be.

After four days of sightseeing in Buenos Aires, we flew on to Cusco, Peru. There we boarded the Belmond Hiram Bingham train—named after an early-twentieth-century American explorer—for the three-hour journey to Machu Picchu, the iconic fifteenth-century Inca sanctuary that is now a UNESCO World Heritage Site. Machu Picchu was stunning, but we spent less than a day exploring and marvelling. This was our whirlwind, check-everything-out vacation. We wanted to at least get the flavour of everything the continent had to offer. I imagined we might return someday to explore it all more deeply.

The next day, we flew to Quito, Ecuador, where we were met by a representative of the La Selva Amazon Lodge. He shepherded us on the next legs of our five-hour journey, by small plane, motorized canoe and kayak, up the Napo River, past Indigenous villages and belching industrial smokestacks and into the Yasuní Biosphere Reserve. Our destination: La Selva's eco-lodge, on a lagoon in the Ecuadorian Amazon rainforest that is inaccessible by road. La Selva bills itself as "a luxury resort in the heart of the rainforest [in] one of the most biodiverse places on Earth, home to literally millions of species of plants, animals, birds and insects." It came as advertised. I can still recall our final kayak ride to the lodge that first night. It was pitch black and rain poured down. We brushed past jungle vines hanging over the river and heard the spooky sounds of unfamiliar animals off in the distance. At one point, I looked over towards Gerry, and there, sitting next to him on a leaf, was a gigantic tarantula. "Look, Gerry," I said, marvelling, pointing. He took a look.

"Oh, all right," was all he said.

While Gerry, it is fair to say, was never much of a fan of nature, he became even more distracted, distanced, more in his own world, as our trip progressed. Or perhaps I am rearranging my memories of his mood based on what I learned later. Regardless, I have flash memories from those days.

One morning, after a jungle walk with a guide and a small group, we were returning to the lodge when a guide approached us excitedly to tell us one of the staff had seen an anaconda, the world's largest snake, and we should all hop in a canoe to go see it.

"I really have to work," Gerry said. He was antsy, moving his feet as if he was already heading back to the lodge. "I have to get on my computer." The guide looked at Gerry in disbelief, explaining just how rare it is to see an anaconda up close. But whatever Gerry had to do on his computer that morning, it must have been more pressing, because he just shook his head, turned and walked towards our lodge.

* * *

"UGH." GERRY NEVER SWORE. *Ugh* was his all-purpose, go-to exclamation when he was stressed or frustrated. And now he was stressed *and* frustrated. "There's a problem with one of my payment processors," he announced out of the blue one day. "CIBC's frozen some of their accounts. I've got to deal with it."

By this point, we were in the worst possible place for a crisis—in the Pacific Ocean, off the Galapagos Islands, nearly a thousand kilometres offshore from Ecuador. We weren't scheduled to fly back to the mainland—and stable internet service—for another few days. Gerry had been so worried about the lack of connectivity at sea that, before we left Nova Scotia, he'd purchased a satellite box that looked like CIA spyware. It came with its own black suitcase. Even with it, Gerry needed to climb up to the ship's top deck and angle the dish in a particular way to get spotty reception.

The Galapagos cruise was supposed to be one of the highlights of our trip—a seven-night sail aboard a sixteen-passenger Celebrity Xploration luxury cruise ship around the famous, isolated archipelago of volcanic islands that straddle the equator and are home to all sorts of plant, land and sea species found nowhere else on Earth. Three ocean currents collide there, creating a unique mix of warm and cold waters that spawn crystal-clear turquoise water that laps against coloured sand beaches.

I had been keener to see the Galapagos than Gerry, who invariably preferred urban civilization—Japan, Hong Kong, Singapore—to the off-the-grid natural beauty these remote islands offer. He'd agreed to our Galapagos adventure mostly to please me. But now, he was growing increasingly agitated.

One night, after an enjoyable dinner with some people we'd met on the cruise, Gerry went up to the top deck to try again to get an internet connection, and I went back to our room. But I'd had too much to drink, and the ship itself was rolling in the rough waters. Coming out of the bathroom, I tripped over the step and fell. I ended up with a massive bruise on my leg. When Gerry finally returned to our cabin, I tried to explain what had happened. Usually, Gerry, who always drank more than me, would have been sympathetic. This time, he snapped, "Well, maybe you shouldn't have drunk so much." That may not seem like a big deal, but it was so out of character for Gerry that I was taken aback. I could never remember Gerry being angry with me, so when he was, it was shocking, a sign of just how much stress he must be under.

His stress stressed me out.

We talked. "You know what?" he said. "I just really want to go home." After the cruise, we'd been scheduled to spend two nights in a hotel on Baltra, one of the islands in the Galapagos, to celebrate my birthday, then fly to Quito and, from there, make our way back to Halifax. I cancelled our reservations and rebooked us on the first flights back home.

"You're sure you don't mind?" he said, his calm returning. "It's your birthday."

Though I didn't fully comprehend why he was so upset, it was clear he had been near his breaking point. "Don't worry about that," I said. "You need to go home. We're going home."

5

Castles in the Cloud

G erry and I began discussing the idea of getting married almost from the time we moved in together. I knew soon after I met him that I wanted to be Gerry's wife. Despite what had happened between Jacob and me, and even with my own parents, I still believed in the *idea* of marriage, the notion you could form a bond with another person that was so strong and significant and special that you were ready, willing and able to exchange forever vows. I felt that bond with Gerry.

Gerry was . . . well, less enthusiastic. He didn't exactly oppose marriage, but he framed it differently. "If you want to get married," he would say, "I do, too."

Neither of us, however, considered marriage to be that inevitable next step on an inexorable path leading to children. Certainly not then, and perhaps not ever. We were just twenty-six when we met. We were both keen to travel; there was way too much world we wanted to experience for ourselves before we would even consider bringing children into it. That's because we understood that if we did have children, they would have to become our priority. Children need routine. They need parents to take them to soccer games on Tuesdays, gymnastics on Thursdays, be there for them in good times and bad. Were we ready then to give up the self-satisfying lifestyle we had created for ourselves, and were enjoying to the fullest, to make room for children? Could we—*should* we—take a baby with us on our travels? Would either of us ever be comfortable home-schooling a child aboard the *Gulliver* while sailing around the Caribbean?

The answers in that moment were no, no and no. But we didn't consider it a forever decision. We agreed we would revisit the question of beginning a family when we were thirty-five. The timing wasn't about some ticking biological clock; in fact, I was more interested in adopting a child, perhaps from India or China, than giving birth to a baby. Gerry liked—or, at least, acquiesced to—that idea, too. Children would come, if they came, after we'd seen more of the world, after we'd built our dream home on our island, after Gerry's bitcoin business had become less hectic and he was able to delegate more of its day-to-day duties to others. That, at least, was the plan.

I wasn't surprised when Gerry formally asked me to marry him. Though we hadn't told anyone, we had already decided on a venue and had even settled on the wedding date. But the idea of choosing an engagement ring flustered Gerry.

"What kind of ring do you want?" he asked. Gerry wasn't comfortable making certain decisions—where to eat, where to travel, what to wear. "I wish I could just wear the same pants and the same shirt every day," he would say, "and only have to make decisions about big things." Getting married might have been a big decision, but choosing an engagement ring didn't engage his interest. So I sent him some photos featuring different styles I liked.

Then he wanted to know, "How much should a ring cost?" I explained that the generally accepted rule in Wedding World is that a man should spend three months' salary on his bride's engagement ring. Gerry started to laugh. "That's not going to happen!" At the time, he told me, he was earning $10 million a month.

The ring he ended up buying—online, of course, from an ethically sourced Canadian jewellery site called Brilliant Earth—was a stunningly beautiful, round, two-carat diamond ring. Truth? Gerry didn't choose it; I did. I liked its small band because my fingers are small, and the round shape was popular at the time. "I like the look of this one," I told him. Then Gerry went to work, researching the carat, the colour and the cut.

Despite my involvement in buying the ring, Gerry did manage to surprise me with a very traditional proposal. One beautiful sunny day in August 2017, he suggested we go for a sail aboard the *Gulliver* and enjoy a picnic lunch. I can't remember how he got me out to the bow of the yacht, but once there, he dropped to one knee just like in the movies and presented me with the ring. "You're my best friend," he told me. "Will you marry me?"

I smiled, dizzy with happiness, and thought, *How lucky am I?* The man of my dreams had just proposed to me with a beautiful ring on the bow of *our yacht!* It felt like we were living in our own real-life fairy tale.

Now that we had made it official, we could tell our families and our friends. Which led to the first complication.

During our travels that spring, we'd had dinner at the Ashford, once the 350-acre family estate of the Guinness family, now the oldest castle hotel in Ireland. Over the years, the Ashford's guest list had included everyone from John Wayne to Brad Pitt, Oscar Wilde to John Lennon. "This is so amazing," I said to Gerry as we walked around the sprawling grounds with its landscaped gardens, ancient woodlands and even an emerald lake. "I've always dreamed of getting married in a castle."

"Well," Gerry said, transforming himself into wish-fulfilling Gerry again, "why don't we get married in a castle?"

In the end, however, the Ashford seemed just too big for the wedding we had in mind. "Let's find a smaller castle," Gerry suggested. I soon settled on Inverlochy, a Scottish castle hotel that came highly recommended by *A Lady in London*, a British blog I followed. We booked Inverlochy for October 8, 2018—those eights again! Our plan was that we would immediately follow the wedding celebration with an amazing honeymoon adventure worthy of our castle wedding.

But now that we could tell our friends about our plans, we discovered that Aly, my best friend since junior high, had already made arrangements to marry her fiancé, Kyle, on October 20 in Nova Scotia, and she wanted me to be one of her bridesmaids. That meant we would need to return from Scotland almost immediately after our own wedding to take part in Aly's pre-wedding festivities. I didn't want to miss any of that, either! But what about *our* honeymoon?

In the end, Gerry and I decided we would get married legally in a private backyard ceremony in Fall River on June 8, 2018 (of course), with just Aly and Kyle as witnesses, then turn our Scottish wedding into a family celebration, followed by a mini-honeymoon in Amsterdam. After that, we would fly back to Nova

Scotia for Aly's wedding and organize the extended honeymoon of our dreams for later in 2018.

GERRY'S FACE was pale, his body stiff. His hands clutched at the bedsheets. I had never seen him like that before; I wouldn't see him that way again until we were in India, nearly six months later. It was early July 2018, and Gerry lay on the bed in a hotel room in Bath, England.

"Are you OK?" I demanded, my concern rising.

"I don't know what's wrong," he answered, his voice soft. But he *did* know what was wrong. And why he was in such pain now.

The year before we met—after Gerry had been diagnosed with Crohn's disease following an attack so severe, he was hospitalized—he'd been put on a medication called Remicade, an artificial antibody originally developed from mice. Remicade reduces symptoms in patients like Gerry with "moderately to severely active" Crohn's who haven't responded well to other treatments. Every eight weeks, Gerry had to go to a local infusion clinic for a maintenance dose of the drug. Over the course of two to three hours, the medication would be slowly injected into his body through an IV in his arm, giving him another two months of relatively pain-free living. It had worked for Gerry, and we had long since learned to plan our travels around his treatment schedule.

But now it seemed the medication's mitigating effect was not lasting as long as it had. During this episode in the middle of our most recent trip, Gerry agreed to see a doctor who prescribed Prednisone, an anti-inflammatory steroid, to control his flare-up until we could get home to Nova Scotia. It helped. But not much.

We'd arrived in Bath near the tail end of what had been a four-week trip to celebrate my mother's sixty-fifth birthday. Gerry and I had flown my mom and my stepdad, Tom, in the private jet to Iceland, where we spent a few days together before boarding a commercial flight to Paris to mark her actual birthday, and then we all flew on to Greece for a vacation. Gerry and I left them in Athens and caught a flight to Scotland so we could finally inspect the castle I'd booked, sight unseen, almost a year before. After that, Gerry and I drove back to London, then on to Bath. Our plan was to spend a day at Stonehenge, the prehistoric stone monuments that date to 3,000 BC and have become among the most famous landmarks in the United Kingdom, and then return home to Canada.

But now, Gerry was on the bed in obvious pain. "We don't have to go to Stonehenge," I told him.

Gerry insisted. "I want you to see it. I've already seen it, but I want you to see it." In the end, Gerry drove our rental car to

Stonehenge, but he was in such pain, he told me he would wait in the car while I did the tour. "Are you sure?" I kept asking. "We can see it together some other time."

"No, no," he said again. "I want you to go."

Gerry remained in constant pain the rest of the trip. By September, when we were back in Nova Scotia, already-skinny Gerry had dropped thirty pounds. He had a colonoscopy, but the scope didn't seem to tell doctors much that was helpful. Driving him home after the procedure, I couldn't help myself. I started to cry. "I'm just so worried about you," I said through my tears.

He looked at me then, still doped up from the medication, with those all-loving eyes. "It's so sweet of you to be so worried about me, but you don't have to worry. I'm fine."

I KNEW enough about Crohn's by then to understand that stress, while it doesn't cause Crohn's, can make it much worse. And Gerry had been under unrelenting pressure since that moment six months before, when he learned that CIBC had frozen $30 million worth of Quadriga's clients' funds.

Unsurprisingly, customers complained; many demanded to cash out their Quadriga holdings. That only made the situation worse for Gerry, much worse than I knew. I didn't know, for example, that in March 2018, CIBC emailed Gerry, asking to speak with him directly. He declined, telling them to put their questions in writing. When they did—the questions were about Quadriga's relationship with two professional payment processors—Gerry simply didn't respond. But clients—their confidence in Quadriga shaken by CIBC's actions at the very moment the value of cryptocurrency went into free fall—began to desert the platform in droves.

Whenever Gerry talked to me about what was going on, he blamed all his troubles on CIBC. "They're holding my customers' money that I've already paid out to them, so now I'm trying to float Quadriga $30 million of my own money to cover it," he would say. "I just feel like saying to Quadriga's customers, 'Whatever, guys. Get your own money.'" He sounded so frustrated, so aggrieved. And I believed him.

Before CIBC happened, we'd already decided to spend the winter of 2018 at our new house in Kelowna, but that only made a bad situation worse. When we were in Nova Scotia, thanks to the time-zone difference, Gerry's workday began well before many of his Toronto clients and business associates even woke up. "I'm an hour ahead of everybody," he used to brag. Kelowna was the opposite, and worse. By the time it was nine o'clock in the morning in British Columbia, it was already noon in Toronto.

So much was happening in Toronto, where Quadriga had filed a lawsuit to force CIBC to free up its funds, that Gerry felt he was constantly running just to keep up with developments.

Gerry had always been a workaholic, but now he never looked up from his laptop. He just sat at the table in the kitchen, hunched over his computer, typing so fast, so focused on the screen, as if it might hold the answers to his questions. He rarely slept. The more stressed he became, the less he wanted anyone around who might disturb him. Although we'd had a maid in Fall River who came regularly to clean, I took on all the housework in Kelowna so he wouldn't have to cope with an outsider. But there were many days when he barely spoke even to me. I'd wake up, go to the gym, come home, run my Halifax property management company from my office in our house in Kelowna, trying to stay out of Gerry's way while also being there for him to vent. I desperately wanted to do more, but it seemed there was nothing more I could do.

Gerry had begun drinking more, too, which only exacerbated his Crohn's. Gerry and I had always enjoyed drinking. A sociable glass or two of wine here, a drink at the end of the day there. But it had always been controlled, disciplined. "Never a pour before four." But I could sense his drinking now had begun to be less about relaxing and more about relieving tensions. Sometimes, in the afternoons, when he would go to the old-fashioned bar cart we'd set up in our Kelowna house and begin to make a martini, I'd ask him, "Is your stomach sore?"

"Yeah," he'd answer, "a bit." But he kept on pouring.

The good news was that Gerry's doctors had come up with an alternative medication to treat his Crohn's. Stelara, a fully human monoclonal immunoglobulin antibody that helps reduce intestinal inflammation, had only recently been approved as a treatment for Crohn's. The best news from Gerry's perspective was that he could administer Stelara himself rather than needing to go to the infusion clinic.

A few days before we left for India, in fact, we were sitting in our bedroom, chatting, surrounded by suitcases waiting to be packed. I looked over at Gerry, who was about to stick a needle in his leg.

"I don't know if I could stab myself with a needle," I told him.

"I just really hope that this starts to make me feel better," Gerry answered as he stuck the needle in, "because I still don't really feel all that good."

"WHERE SHOULD we go for your birthday?" I'd asked, hoping travel might cheer Gerry up. It was April, and we were now back in Nova Scotia.

Gerry and I had turned our respective birthdays into occasions for ever more spectacular new adventures. We'd celebrated my twenty-eighth birthday in Dubai, and my twenty-ninth during our first six-week vacation in Southeast Asia. We marked Gerry's twenty-ninth birthday during a four-week trip to Greece, Italy and Malta. We were in Greece for his actual birthday, and I struggled to figure out what to get him. He didn't need anything, and anything he wanted, he could buy. So I looked for an experience we could share. In the end, I surprised him by renting a large catamaran to take us around the Greek island of Mykonos. We went swimming off the side of the vessel and then had a huge barbecue feast at the end of the day to celebrate. As always, Gerry would have preferred to be on his own and was uncomfortable being served by others. When it came time to eat, Gerry invited the crew to join us for our meal.

It had been Gerry's idea to add Malta to our itinerary that year. Located south of Italy, Malta is the world's tenth-smallest country, but is also a member of the European Union. Since 2014, Malta had begun granting citizenship under a controversial "golden passport" scheme that gave not only a Maltese passport, but also a European Union one to almost anyone willing to invest more than $1 million (Canadian) in the country, buy property and live there at least briefly. Almost anyone, it turned out, often included criminals and shady characters from all over. Gerry didn't mention any of that to me. He just said he was keen to get his European Union passport for business reasons and that Malta would be the easiest route to that end. The purpose for our stopover there was to figure out if we liked the place and whether we could find a property we wanted to buy. We loved the hotel where we stayed in St. Julian's Bay and considered buying a house or condo nearby. "We'll just bring Nitro and Gully, and live in our property in Malta until we get our European citizenship," Gerry suggested. But so far we hadn't followed up on that scheme. So far.

So, I asked him now, where should we go for his thirtieth birthday on May 11? "Let's just book the Bahamas," Gerry said flatly. The Bahamas? We'd been there a number of times before; it had become a kind of go-to destination for short breaks. But for a landmark birthday?

"Just the Bahamas?" I asked.

"Yeah," he answered. "I just want to go to the Bahamas."

I knew he was busy and stressed, knew a court date had been set for June to hear his suit against CIBC, knew we could get excellent internet in the Bahamas, knew we could fly there and back quickly if need be.

"OK," I said. We'd have plenty of years ahead for birthday adventures.

* * *

WITH GERRY FACING ever-ratcheting tensions at Quadriga and me trying to manage Robertson Nova's growing property portfolio—and both of us still keen to spend as much time as possible seeing the world—I realized we needed help. In February 2018, I contacted our realtor, Jill Hann, to get permission to approach her assistant, Tanya Reid, to take on some freelance work for me on a per-hour basis. Tanya, a take-charge self-starter, not only understood the real estate business inside and out, but she had also been directly involved when I'd bought each of my rental properties. During that process, we'd connected professionally and personally. Tanya fit in seamlessly, taking over our day-to-day bookkeeping and developing a more efficient financial management system, doing it all part time. I was impressed. I didn't have enough work to justify a full-time assistant, but . . .

Gerry and I were on our back deck on a September afternoon, drinking wine and chatting about our day, when I broached my idea. "What if we 'stole' Tanya from Jill and made her a full-time assistant, working for both of us?"

Gerry was . . . Gerry. He laughed. "Do it," he said. So I did. In the end, Tanya became primarily a personal assistant for Gerry, picking up laundry and running errands, while Gerry continued to run the business as he always had—alone, from inside his laptop.

* * *

GERRY AND I rarely fought. When we did, it was almost always about something inconsequential. We'd have one too many drinks and one of us would say something about some small thing and that would escalate. At some point, I might raise my voice, and Gerry would inevitably end up crying.

"Sweetheart," he would say finally through his tears, "I don't know why you're mad at me." And then he would go to bed without another word. I always felt awful. Although I knew even then that there was clearly another darker, more ruthless Gerry—a man who claimed he didn't need friends, who would easily cut off relations with any business associate who crossed him—the Gerry I lived with and loved was a passive, loving person who almost never uttered a cross word in my direction and would cry if I hurt his feelings. The best part about our arguments was that they rarely lasted beyond a good night's sleep.

Our only real arguments over matters that mattered had to do with his family, mostly Cheryl. Perhaps the tensions between Cheryl and me were as inevitable—and as cliché—as those between any mother-in-law and the woman who'd married her son. There were also good times; we both loved to travel, and Cheryl and I could spend hours together, poring over travel books, sharing our itineraries and discussing next destinations. In December 2017, before Gerry and I left for our cruise around

South America—his mother and father later enjoyed their own Galapagos vacation—we flew to Belleville for a pre-Christmas celebration. I bought funny, ugly Christmas sweaters for everyone to wear. It was a fun time, in part because—as Cheryl herself told me—while Gerry and his family tended to be reserved, I brought a larger-than-life personality to every occasion. "You've brought the fun back into family gatherings," she said.

Cheryl claimed to "adore" me, but we had our differences.

When Gerry and I suggested we might decide not to have children, Cheryl breezed past our doubts. "You'll change your minds," she said flatly. To be fair, Cheryl could sometimes surprise me. I'd been reluctant to tell her that Gerry and I had decided to fund an orphanage in India, worried she would denigrate the idea. Instead, she embraced it. "That is so cool," she said. "Just awesome."

In September 2017, during a long weekend in Las Vegas, we finally told Gerry's parents we were getting married. Waiting for more than a month after we got engaged to share our news with them had been Gerry's idea. He liked his secrets, liked his control. When I showed them my engagement ring, Cheryl's immediate response was "Now, *that's* a ring."

Still, given the backdrop, I was not surprised when our family castle wedding did not turn out to be the dream event I'd envisioned and I ended up crying angry tears on my own wedding night. But what did surprise—and please—me was Gerry's reaction.

We had decided our Scottish wedding would be a "limited," family-only affair: just my mother and Tom, Cheryl and Bruce, Brad and Jess. We didn't even invite my father; I knew that putting him and my mom in the same room would be inviting problems. I didn't invite my brother or sister, either. And I didn't ask any of my friends; we were already planning another long weekend in the Bahamas with them in November. As for Gerry's friends, he didn't have any, or even seem to want or need them.

But our small numbers made it impossible not to notice what seemed to me like Cheryl's unhappiness about everything. I had even planned fun activities for us, including our own version of Highland games. The games were too hard, Cheryl said. Nothing seemed to please her. "Oh my God," I wanted to scream. We had paid for everyone to fly to Scotland, paid for everyone's stay at Inverlochy. "You're in a castle. How much more up to par can it get?"

Maybe it was just the inevitable tensions that come with a wedding but, in the end, Cheryl and Bruce left the castle early, only informing Gerry they were gone by text. Gerry's reaction: "I'm going to tell my mother she's not welcome anymore." It might have been just an in-the-moment reaction—and I would never have asked that of Gerry—but in that moment, it was exactly the right thing to say, and it made me love him even more.

THE WEEK before we were to leave for India, we flew to the Bahamas in the jet with Aly and Kyle, and two other couples we knew. It was partly a chance to celebrate our marriage once again and partly a fun way to spend a weekend with friends—dining, drinking, playing in the water park, swimming in the ocean—at the Atlantis resort and casino on Paradise Island. Because we could.

Before we left, Gerry warned me—so that I would warn the others—not to bring cannabis or any other recreational drugs with them on the trip. Although Canada had legalized cannabis the month before, it was still illegal in the Bahamas. Gerry, who didn't smoke weed himself and would never purchase illegal drugs of any sort, became adamant to the point of paranoia, even suggesting at one point that we not take the others with us because one of them might ignore his request and be arrested. "It'd be really bad," he said.

Looking back now, the moment seems even stranger. Did Gerry create his buttoned-down, law-abiding, righteous persona just for me, or was there something more complicated and nuanced happening inside his head?

Earlier that spring, while we were still living in British Columbia, we spent the Easter weekend cross-country skiing with friends in Canmore, Alberta. Gerry overheard one of them complaining about the visitors' fee at the nearby national park and suggesting she'd sneak in rather than pay the fee. Gerry didn't treat it as a joke. "That's stealing," he complained to me later. "You shouldn't sneak into a park, because it's wrong. We wouldn't have parks if people refused to pay for them."

Was this Real Gerry? Or just the Gerry he wanted me to believe in? I don't know.

In February 2018, in the early stages of what would become our own *annus horribilis*, I suggested to Gerry that we draw up wills. We had all these assets together—the boat, the plane, properties on both coasts, the dogs—and we still weren't married. What if . . . ?

Gerry agreed, but then everything else happened, and nothing happened with the will. I understood that Gerry was too distracted to focus on unlikely what-ifs, so I backed off. We did talk about the idea again in June, right after our wedding. This time, Gerry raised the subject. "We should probably get that will," he said. But we didn't.

Then, in early November, less than a month before we were to leave for India and our extended honeymoon, my brother, Adam, suffered a serious heart attack that suddenly made what-if much more real and urgent. "Gerry," I said, "we're getting a will."

Although he was still too worried about his own issues to seriously contemplate what might happen in the event that one or both of us should die, he acknowledged my concerns. "OK," he allowed, "I can see why you think it's important."

I contacted a lawyer I'd worked with on a property deal, and she sorted out most of the details by email. We would be each other's executors. If we both died at the same time or were unable to take on the executor's duties, we identified who should take our place. Gerry named Brad and Jess as next in line. If not them, my childhood friend Anne, one of my closest and most responsible friends.

Essentially, we left everything we owned, jointly or individually, to each other. That included, in Gerry's case, "all my property, both real and personal, of every nature and kind and wheresoever situate, including any property over which I may have a general power of appointment, including all digital assets." Even his frequent flyer points.

Deciding what to do with individual assets if we both died turned out to be almost as easy. We would bequeath our Kelowna house to Brad and Jess, along with Gerry's 2017 Lexus and his Cessna. Bruce and Cheryl would inherit both the *Gulliver* and our island. My mother and Tom would get my company. My father and his twin sister, Debbie, who'd been like a mother to me, would be the beneficiaries of the Fall River house and lake properties, as well as our dogs, Nitro and Gully, along with $100,000 for their "care and maintenance for the remainder of their lives." We'd loaned my friend Anne and her husband, Alex, money to help them buy their first house in Calgary; that loan would be forgiven if we died. My engagement ring and other jewellery, along with my 2015 Mini Cooper, would be bequeathed to Aly. "All remaining motor vehicles" Gerry then owned, including his Tesla, would be passed on to my brother, Adam, and sister, Kim. Easy.

After the lawyer turned her notes into a draft will, she called to set up a time for us to meet and go over the details. I mentioned that we were leaving for India soon and would sign it when we returned. She quickly responded with an email: "You have to come in and sign this before you go to India. You've given me directions for your will, but you have not signed it. This is not good. You have to come in."

We did. During the course of the conversation, the lawyer asked Gerry, "What about your business?"

"No, not my business." He was adamant. "We just want the will to cover our basic personal assets." Gerry had been annoyed in a generic way since even before we arrived at the lawyer's office that day, beginning when he had trouble finding a parking space. I put his mood down to that, to his general stress level, to the fact he didn't like thinking about death. I did know just how concerned Gerry was about his safety and his health whenever we travelled. Perhaps that was it. But not including the business?

"Well, you really should," the lawyer tried again, emphasizing how integral the business was, how many of Gerry's assets appeared to be tied up in Quadriga.

Gerry didn't budge. "No, I'm not putting the company in the will. If I die, the company dies with me."

Later, after we left the lawyer's office, Gerry tried to explain. "I'm the only one with all the banking connections, all the connections with the bitcoin accounts and all the payment processors. No one else knows it. It would just not run without me."

I wasn't sure I understood, but if that's the way he wanted it, I was OK with it.

Just as I was OK with his equally odd refusal to buy life insurance. "Life insurance is just in case something terrible happens," he told me. "If I die, Jen, you'll have $5 million in your bank account, plus another $12 million in properties. I think you'll be fine for money."

I wouldn't be. But I didn't know that then, didn't have a clue. Neither, I'm sure, did Gerry.

On November 27, 2018, we each signed our last will and testament. Four days later, we left for India.

WE'D ONLY been in India for a few days when the news arrived from Canada. On December 3, 2018, the Ontario Superior Court ruled that most of the $30 million worth of Quadriga client funds CIBC had frozen for a full year "shall be immediately released."

The next day, Gerry sent out a celebratory message to Quadriga customers. "Much to our delight, the judge has ruled in our favour and the funds are being released," he wrote. "According to our counsel, the funds should be paid out by the end of this week. We thank everyone for their support as we have dealt with the most challenging time in our company's history. Now that we can put this situation behind us, we look forward to focusing on improving our services and offering a better cryptocurrency trading experience for Canadians."

Gerry was ecstatic. So was I—for him, and for us. I realized how stressed I'd been because Gerry was so stressed. A weight had been lifted from both of us. *Everything is going to get better now,* I thought.

6

A Death in India

But nothing got better. Instead, everything had become worse, much worse. Now, less than a week later, we were in our hotel room in the Oberoi Rajvilas in Jaipur, Gerry on the bed as ill as I'd ever seen him. I called the front desk. "I need an ambulance," I said urgently. "My husband is sick, and we need to go to the best hospital." I kept repeating "best hospital."

"No problem," the voice at the other end of the line responded calmly. "We're going to send someone to get you."

But there was a problem. Gerry was wearing jeans; he told me he needed to change into something looser and more comfortable for the trip to the hospital. His pyjama pants were in his suitcase, and I couldn't seem to open it. At some point, I assume, someone had wrapped one of those little plastic security rings around the suitcase opening. I had no scissors or knife to open it. Finally, I remembered my own suitcase was already open. I urgently rummaged through it and found a huge pair of sweats I'd bought at Walmart so that I could be super-comfortable when we were in private. I offered them to Gerry and helped him change.

By this point, Gerry couldn't walk. Three small, young men from the hotel arrived at our villa, lifted him up and gently placed him in a golf cart for the drive to where I expected the ambulance would be waiting.

While I walked beside them, I called my sister-in-law, Jess. She was a medical resident back in Ontario. More importantly, she'd grown up with Gerry and Brad in Belleville and had been there for Gerry's whole Crohn's journey, from his diagnosis six years earlier. I explained everything that was going on.

"You know what?" she said calmly. "It actually sounds like food poisoning."

"I'm scared."

"You're doing all the right things," she reassured me.

"Are you sure? He's telling me he's in such severe pain."

"I have people like that coming into the ER all the time. They're writhing in pain, they're on the floor—and it's food poisoning."

We arrived beside the hotel's SUV. "Where's the ambulance?" I asked.

"No ambulance," the general manager said. "It's India. We'd wait forever for an ambulance. We will drive your husband to the hospital ourselves." The manager, a tall, well-dressed young man, had greeted us when we checked into the hotel. He'd congratulated us on our marriage. And now? An hour later? It all seemed unreal.

With Gerry moaning in the back of the SUV, the manager navigated Jaipur's overcrowded, darkened downtown streets, past the tuk-tuks and motorcycles, around sidewalk vendors and pedestrians, even cows. We were trying to rush to the hospital, but we couldn't because there were cows in front of the car! It was surreal, and now I was panicking. The whole time, Gerry, no longer the stoic, kept asking, "How much longer? How much longer?"

As the manager drove, he talked to hospital officials on his mobile in a mix of English and another language, possibly Punjabi, filling them in on Gerry's condition. I sat beside him in the front seat as he relayed their questions—*Has Gerry had surgeries? What about this? What about that?*—and then he repeated my answers back to them. I told them what Jess had said about food poisoning, but I also informed them Gerry had Crohn's disease. The manager kept repeating what I said, though I wasn't certain that what I said was getting through to whoever was on the other end of the phone.

It took us over half an hour to drive from the hotel to Fortis Escorts Hospital, a modern private hospital where the hotel had arranged for Gerry to be seen. Jess googled it and pronounced it OK. I learned later from its website that Fortis boasts it is one of the best hospitals in the region, part of a chain that is a "veritable torch bearer of super specialty centres of excellence across the country."

By the time we arrived, more than half a dozen medical personnel were waiting by the main entrance. They transferred Gerry to a gurney and began giving him medications. The manager kept telling the doctors, "His doctor in Canada thinks it's just food poisoning." And the doctors were saying to each other, "She's his Canadian doctor. She's his family. She knows it's just food poisoning." But was it? I'd never seen Gerry in this kind of pain from food poisoning. I asked Gerry if he would talk to Jess on the phone, describe what he was feeling, but he said he couldn't. "I am in severe pain," was the best he could manage.

I was crying. I couldn't stop. I knew I should be his advocate, maybe demand an X-ray, but I didn't know what he needed. And the doctors kept scolding me, telling me to calm down, that everything would be OK.

Jess said so, too. I was still talking to her on the phone. She was reassuring, saying I was doing everything right, it was just food poisoning and I was overreacting. But I was all alone in a country where I'd never been, in a hospital where I knew no one, so I needed her to validate everything. I got the doctors to give me a printout of the medicines they were giving Gerry and sent it to her. She said that was exactly what she would have prescribed.

By then, we were in the emergency room. At this point, Gerry was its only patient. I looked around. Everything seemed bright and modern, and I felt reassured. And hopeful. After a while, Gerry seemed to calm down. I wasn't sure if that was because of the medicines the doctors had given him or because my Ativan pill—I took them for anxiety, and Gerry had asked for one before we left for the hospital—had finally kicked in.

At some point, a gastroenterologist came to see Gerry. I was glad I was there. "Have you had any previous surgeries?" he asked.

Gerry answered no. "Gerry," I said, "yes, you have. You had a fistula, and they had to fix that." I knew a fistula, an abnormal opening that forms in the wall of the intestine, is common among people with Crohn's, so I thought the doctors would want to know about his surgery.

"Everything's important," the doctor agreed.

After he left, I said to Gerry, "Why would you lie to the doctor?

It doesn't make any sense." It struck me, not for the first time, that Gerry could sometimes act in ways that only made sense to Gerry. Later, another doctor asked me if Gerry drank alcohol, and I said, "Yes, all the time." The doctor was visibly upset; he'd asked Gerry the same question and been told he rarely drank.

The doctors decided to keep him overnight, so the hotel arranged for us to have a private room in the hospital with a cot for me. I didn't even have to ask. It was almost like they knew what I needed before I knew I needed it. Since we were already paying $800 a night for our hotel room, everyone understood we could afford whatever it cost.

Gerry, who was now in the private room and hooked up to an IV, kept saying he had to throw up, so I offered to help him to the bathroom. "I'd rather do it by myself," he said—that was so Gerry—but then he admitted, "I can't hold the IV." So, I helped him; I held the IV for him as he navigated from the hospital bed to the bathroom. After he threw up, I even took pictures of his vomit and sent those to Jess, too. She said his vomit looked "absolutely fine." That reassured me. But later, when I tried to put a blanket over him, Gerry screamed in pain because his stomach hurt so badly, he couldn't stand to even have the blanket touch him.

* * *

THE NEXT MORNING, while Gerry waited for X-rays, someone from the hotel—an assistant manager, I think—came to see me. "Would you like a ride back to the hotel, to get anything, have a shower?" I would. I hadn't slept all night. Doctors and nurses had been in and out of Gerry's room, putting medications in his IV. And I was up frequently myself, helping Gerry to and from the bathroom. To make matters worse, the cot the hospital had provided was small and uncomfortable and came with a scratchy brown blanket. The doctors had already said they wanted to keep Gerry one more night to make sure he was OK and not dehydrated, so I knew I wouldn't sleep the next night, either. A nap in a bed that wasn't a cot sounded appealing. I could take a nap, have a shower, wash my hair and, oh, yes, bring Gerry back his laptop.

Gerry desperately wanted his laptop, which he'd left behind in the hotel room. Even in the midst of all his pain, he'd insisted he needed it with him. He never went anywhere without it, even on our cruises. Last night in the hospital had been the longest he'd ever been apart from it.

Back at the hotel, I gathered his stuff—he needed a change of clothes—and his laptop. The hotel had told me someone would drive me back to the hospital at 1:30 in the afternoon, so I was still in the middle of doing my hair, straightening it to look at least half-decent for Gerry, when I suddenly felt a wave of anxiety wash over me. *This doesn't feel right . . . I should be back there.* I sent him a text: "Hi sweetheart . . . Booboo, please answer, so I know you're OK."

After a while, he texted me back a heart. "They rxated me," he said, mistyping *X-ray*.

I knew the drive to the hospital would take at least half an hour. I had just gotten into the car when he texted again: "They are moving [me] somewhere else because my heart rate is fast and my intestines may be blocked."

"OK, I'm coming."

"I think it's just fast 'cause the X-ray freaked me out."

I texted him a series of questions: "Did they see a blockage? Where are they moving you? Why did the X-ray freak you out?"

He didn't answer. Just: "Cool. They'll tell you where I am." And then: "It's chaos, lol."

"Are you OK, baby?" I texted back, willing the driver to go faster, the traffic to disappear. Everything seemed to move so slowly, almost as though a very heavy blanket had been draped over everything. "What's chaos?" I asked him "What's happening? Baby."

"I think so," he texted in response to my earlier text about whether he was OK. "Just Indian people struggling to drive my bed." I assumed he meant that orderlies were moving him some-where.

"I'm sick with worry," I replied, and more questions came tumbling out of my iPhone: "Did the X-ray or sonogram show anything? Have you spoken to the doctor? Do you feel a lot more pain? So they are only moving you because of your heart rate?"

"I don't mean to pepper you with questions, sweet angel," I added finally. "I'm just worried sick about you."

"Ya, I think," he replied enigmatically. Nothing more.

"I'm eight minutes away from you," I wrote.

And then, a few minutes later: "I'm here and I'm trying to find you, baby."

WHEN I FINALLY pushed through the swinging doors and into the hospital's intensive care unit, the first person I saw was Gerry. He was in a bed on the far wall, facing me, an oxygen mask covering his face. I could see through the clear glass of the mask that he was blue around his lips; his fingertips had bluish tinges, too. I knew that must not be good. I ran over to him and touched his face. It felt cold.

"Why is he so cold?" I yelled, not sure who I was asking, just wanting to make sure someone knew.

Gerry was struggling to breathe. I could see it in his eyes. He was really, really scared.

"What's happening?" he asked, his voice weak.

"I don't know, but I'm going to find out," I said. "I'm not going to leave you . . . I love you."

He took off his mask and said, "I love you, too."

Those were the last words we ever spoke to one another. Looking back now, I feel lucky we got to say we loved each other.

After that, everything blurred: doctors and nurses rushed in and out in their burgundy scrubs, flip-flops on their feet. I kept thinking, *This is bad! This is bad.* After a while, a doctor came to tell me they believed there must be a hole in Gerry's intestines and that the contents were leaking into his stomach, causing an infection.

In that moment, hearing that, it all became too much. This was *not* food poisoning. This was much more serious. I fainted right there in the middle of the ICU, slamming my head on a metal gurney as I fell, sending medical instruments flying everywhere. I ended up on the floor with people surrounding me, kneeling down, taking care of me. I looked over towards Gerry and saw they'd closed the curtain around him. Someone told me, "You need to step away. You have to be strong, or you'll panic him." Had Gerry seen me faint? Had I made his panic worse?

They led me to a nurse's station to sit down. That's when I saw a doctor turn around and say—and I'll never forget it—"Loss of life is a possibility."

The hotel's assistant manager was still with me, and I kept saying to him, "He's not going to die, right? He's not going to die!"

The doctor who seemed to be in charge of Gerry's case—his name, I later learned, was Dr. Jayant Sharma—showed me his X-ray. It didn't pinpoint where the hole was, he said, so they ordered a CAT scan to help them locate the hole before they began the surgery. The problem was, they couldn't stabilize Gerry enough to do the scan.

"Do you have any of his medical records?" the doctor asked. "That might help."

I called Jess again, and handed her the phone so she could speak to the doctor. I heard her say, "Oh my God, no." I knew now it was much more serious than she'd thought, too. But it was Sunday in Ontario, and Gerry's specialist wasn't available to provide his records. Jess sent me forms to fill out to get access to them; I signed on to my computer and emailed them back.

By then, the general manager of the hotel, the one from the night before, had arrived, too. I didn't know if that was simply the level of service they provided in a luxury hotel in India, or if they knew one of their guests might die.

"I need my parents to be contacted," I told the manager. I had already texted my mother and stepfather the night before to say everyone thought Gerry was suffering from food poisoning. Now, when the manager put them on the phone, I heard my stepdad saying, "No, no, no." I didn't talk with them; I couldn't. Instead, the manager took over, talking first with them, then calling the Canadian embassy and other officials, trying to see if they would waive the usual waiting period for a visa so that my parents could fly to India immediately to help me take care of Gerry.

Even as that discussion was going on, the doctor in charge returned: "He's had a cardiac arrest." Was that why they'd closed the curtain? The doctors had revived him, he told me, but they were still working to get him stabilized.

I DIDN'T UNDERSTAND much about Gerry's business, but I did know it needed constant attention, so, if Gerry wasn't available, he'd want Alex Hanin to know. Alex was Quadriga's "chief architect" and programmer, the one other person who knew everything worth knowing about Quadriga. That was at least something I could do to help Gerry while the doctors worked. I found Alex's number and called him in England.

"It's Jen, and Gerry's really sick," I began as soon as he

answered. "You'll have to keep Quadriga running." I paused, then spoke the words I dared not even think: "I don't know if Gerry's going to make it. They said he might die."

Alex flipped out. "No! He can't die, he can't die." He started screaming at me on the phone to get Gerry to a different hospital, somewhere with better facilities.

At this point, I was already overwhelmed. I had no idea what I should do. I knew I needed to focus on doing everything I could to keep Gerry alive. Did that mean getting him to another hospital? I asked the hotel manager to look into the possibility of chartering an air ambulance to fly Gerry to Singapore. While he inquired about that, I called Jess again.

"Jess, what do you think?"

She considered. "You know, he'll be on an air ambulance with just one doctor. If he goes into cardiac arrest, that's one doctor to try to bring him back. In the ICU, he has all these doctors." I looked around. She was right. "And I would definitely not put him on an air ambulance when he's not stabilized," she added.

At this point, a doctor finally came and brought me back behind the curtain to see Gerry. He told me Gerry had had two more smaller "episodes" since his cardiac arrest. There were wires and tubes everywhere. Gerry still looked blue and sickly, but now he also looked like he was sleeping. His shirt was off, but he was wearing my fucking Walmart sweatpants. He would have hated that.

There were a dozen doctors and nurses around his bed, all taking turns, all trying to revive him. I could see his body going up and down, up and down. The bed had been lowered close to the floor for some reason, and I got down on my knees beside him, near his face. I took his hand in mine. It was cold—not cold as in winter cold, but dead cold. You don't know what that's like until you feel it. I couldn't look up; I just put my head down and kept crying.

And then, at some point—I don't know how long it had been—I felt a tap on my shoulder. I looked up. I saw the heart monitor. It was just like in the movies. There'd been a beep, and now a long, flat line ran across the screen . . . and nothing.

What I saw on the monitor at that moment remains seared into my brain. Gerry's heart had stopped beating, while mine continued to thump in my chest. That was probably the loneliest feeling I've ever had. The love of my life was dead, and my life, as I had known it, was over.

THEY MISSPELLED Gerry's name on the Fortis hospital death certificate. He was listed as "Gerel" William Cotten, aged thirty, married. The official Government of Rajasthan death certificate, issued four days later, mangled his last name as "Cottan." None of these bureaucratic errors should have mattered, but they would all soon become fodder for conspiracy theorists to claim Gerry hadn't died. He had. According to the Fortis certificate, he died at 7:26 p.m. on December 9, 2018. The immediate cause of death was listed as "sudden cardiac arrest," with a final diagnosis of "Septic Shock/Peritonitis/Intestinal Obstruction." "The disease, injury or complication which caused death" was listed as Crohn's disease.

The details didn't matter. Gerry was gone. There would be no orphanage opening, no honeymoon cruise, no rest of the world adventures together, no growing old as one, no more Gerry and me.

THE HOTEL ROOM looked different. The luggage was not where it had been. "This isn't my room," I told the hotel manager. He had driven me back from the hospital and walked me to my room. He'd been very kind; the whole hotel staff had. The manager had even called my mom from the hospital to tell her Gerry had died. He'd called Jess, too. Jess's husband, Brad, was the one who told Gerry's parents.

"This isn't my room," I said again.

"I moved your things," the manager explained gently, "to a more private room." Perhaps he just didn't want the other guests to hear me scream. I hadn't even realized it, but back at the hospital, I'd kept screaming over Gerry's body, touching his chest, trying to—I don't even know—to bring him back to life? "Don't take him away!" I yelled as they pulled his body away from me. They finally ushered me out of the ICU and into a small room nearby, where a volunteer waited, I assumed, to provide comfort to relatives of the dead. She was a lovely older woman with long hair and a warm belly, who just hugged me while I screamed. "He was fine," I kept repeating through my tears, and she kept wiping them away.

Finally, a doctor came into the room and ordered me sharply to "stop screaming!" And I did. I hadn't even realized I was screaming. But hers was the voice of authority, and I stopped.

Now I was back in our hotel room that was no longer ours. I looked over at the luggage. It was all still there, but Gerry wasn't. It was surreal. No one close to me had ever died before. And now Gerry, the love of my life, my best friend, was gone, and I was by myself in a country where I knew no one. But I didn't want to talk with anyone. Not now.

First, I sat down and wrote a note to Gerry:

You died today. I don't know how I'm going to live without you. I miss you so much already. I hope you're somewhere lovely and that there is something past death, as we had so many heated debates about. I still believe there is something more, sweetheart, and I like to think it's some-place beautiful and you are happier there than you are here. I will forever be your wife, your soulmate. I'll never forget you and I'll write you all the time. Please know you were my best friend and I loved you so deeply. I am so proud to be your wife.

Then I poured two glasses of wine—one for Gerry, one for me. I played our wedding song, "Moon River," which is about these two drifters off to see the world. It had always seemed so perfect for us. And then I danced to the music, pretending I was still dancing with Gerry.

7

Dead Man's Switch

It was now December 10, 2018, the morning after Gerry's death, and all I knew was I desperately wanted to be back home in Canada with people I knew and loved, and people who knew and loved Gerry. And I needed to bring Gerry home with me. I wasn't leaving without him.

But the company that was supposed to orchestrate that journey demanded $12,000 (US) upfront. Normally, that would not have been a problem. Gerry had millions of dollars in bank accounts back in Canada; he even told me once he had $10 million in one account with the Canadian Tire Bank (he'd chosen it, he said, because the retail chain's banking arm offered high interest). And I had my own credit cards with limits that would easily cover what the transportation company wanted. But the company wouldn't accept a credit card. It had to be cash or a bank wire.

To complicate all that, it was now Monday morning in India, but still Sunday in Canada.

Finally, I texted Gerry's partner, Alex, in England where it was Monday, too. He would understand how to exchange some of Gerry's bitcoins for cash and wire it to me.

The truth is, I still knew very little about Quadriga, or how bitcoins worked. I didn't even have my own bitcoin account. I hadn't even had any peripheral involvement in the company since I'd stopped processing payments for Gerry in 2016. Quadriga was Gerry's business, and that had been fine with me.

But now Gerry was dead. And I needed cash to get his body home.

"I need $12,000," I told Alex. Alex somehow figured out how to make it happen, and the money arrived at the transportation company. He understood that, after I got back to Halifax, I would send him a cheque to cover it.

Alex's primary interest at that point was Gerry's laptop. "I don't mean to sound insensitive," he told me, "but keep the laptop safe. Don't let it out of your sight, because you're going to need it." I didn't understand what he meant, not then. I had no idea what was actually on the laptop, just that Gerry had always stressed how important it was to running the business. He once called it "the key to the castle." I thought, *I won't let Gerry down. I'll keep the laptop safe.* It hadn't been out of my sight since I brought it with me to the hospital the previous afternoon, and now I resolved to keep it beside me all the way back to Canada.

THANKS TO THE TRANSPORTATION company I'd hired to help facilitate matters and the Canadian embassy, I was booked on an Air Canada flight leaving New Delhi for Toronto at 11 o'clock that night. Which meant I'd have to get from Jaipur to New Delhi, with Gerry's body, in time to connect with that flight.

Before we could even leave Jaipur, however, I had to deal with an insane amount of paperwork. The hotel had very generously waived the room charges for our two nights; I only had to reimburse them for the $1,700 hospital bill, which the hotel had paid upfront.

At first, the transportation company suggested transporting Gerry's body from Jaipur to New Delhi in a refrigerated truck, but I said no. I would have had to make the journey in a separate vehicle, and at that moment in time, I knew I needed to be with him. We agreed the company would charter a small plane to fly Gerry and me to New Delhi together. It was just a one-hour flight.

But before that could happen, I had to go to the morgue to identify Gerry's body. More paperwork. More trauma. More tears. An older woman accompanied me into a small room in the basement of a building—I think it was a university hospital—and the whole scene unfolded just like an episode of *CSI*. There were three drawers, and Gerry's body was in the middle one. Someone pulled it open. Most of his body was covered with a sheet, but I could see his face. It was completely blue. I'll never forget that face, all scrunched up like he was thinking. I couldn't help myself. That blue body had been a real person I'd loved and cherished, his body so warm, and . . . what was he now? I cried in the woman's arms. I was surprised to see that she cried, too. Finally, I said, "Yes, that's him." And they just closed the drawer and put him back in.

I didn't know until later that the woman who headed the anatomy department at Mahatma Gandhi Medical College had refused to embalm Gerry there, partly because hotel staff had brought the body instead of someone from the hospital, and partly because the hotel official who'd transported his body couldn't provide all the information she wanted to know in advance. Had Gerry suffered from AIDS, or cancer, or some other disease? Because the hotel knew I wanted to fly Gerry's body home with me later that day, the embalming was done at SMS Medical College, another smaller institution half an hour away. SMS processed his body and issued an embalming certificate at 3:30 p.m., after which the hotel transported Gerry's body to the Jaipur airport.

I travelled separately in another hotel vehicle to the airport, where I was supposed to connect with Poonam, the woman from the transportation company I'd been dealing with on the phone all day. But for some reason, the hotel driver, after every kind thing the hotel had done for me over the past twenty-four hours, simply dumped me outside the Jaipur airport and drove off. There I was, stranded, alone, trying to manoeuvre my luggage and Gerry's to the airport entrance. There were people everywhere, screaming in what I guessed was Punjabi. Guards stood in front of the entrance, refusing admission to anyone who didn't have a passport and boarding pass. I didn't. Poonam had instructed me to leave Gerry's and my passports at the hotel front desk so she could pick them up and use them to complete the necessary paperwork before returning them to me when we met me at the airport.

Where was Poonam?

I tried texting, but she didn't respond. So, I just stood there, in front of the terminal, tears streaming down my face, feeling totally helpless again.

Finally, a woman approached. "Jennifer," she said in halting English. "It's Poonam."

Poonam was fifty-ish, with a kind-looking face. Almost immediately, however, she turned away from me and began yelling at the guard in words I didn't understand, pointing at me and then yelling some more. I had no clue what she said, but as soon as she showed him our passports, the guard let us pass. Inside, a young woman who worked at the airport helped us navigate a speeded-up journey through all the metal detectors and security screening until, suddenly, we were standing in the intense late-afternoon heat on the tarmac next to a small jet. Gerry's coffin, a simple wooden box covered in black, stapled fabric—not one I would have chosen, certainly not one Gerry would have selected—sat on a gurney beside the plane.

Bizarrely, Poonam and a group of men in orange jackets posed for a photo in front of Gerry's coffin before the men slid it aboard the plane. I should have been offended—it was more than insensitive—but I was beyond feeling by then. I thought, *I don't care. Poonam is helping me get home. And that's all I need to know.*

There were just two seats on the plane: one for me, and one facing me, for Poonam. They slid the coffin in beside us. I placed my hand on it, felt the roughness of the fabric and thought how bizarre it was. A week before, Gerry, very much alive, and I had flown from Canada to India in luxury pods in business class. Now, as we began our return journey, Gerry was still beside me, but no longer alive, his body inside a black box.

Poonam told me she wouldn't normally have come to Jaipur—her office was in New Delhi—"but last night, I saw your file, and I just had this feeling I had to help you. I didn't want you to have to fly with the casket all by yourself." Unceremoniously, she then handed me Gerry's wedding band.

Such an odd woman. At one moment, she could seem so considerate; the next, aloof. While we sat waiting for the plane to take off, in fact, she made business calls on her mobile, laughing, joking with people on the other end. After the plane was airborne and she couldn't talk on her phone any longer, she immediately fell asleep, leaving me alone with the casket she'd said she didn't want me to have to be alone with.

And with my grief and loneliness. I felt so profoundly, so completely alone. At the moment, I wasn't thinking about the future. I couldn't have imagined what was to come.

IN NEW DELHI, a woman from the Canadian embassy met me. Her job, she explained, was to help Canadians abroad who needed assistance. She seemed warm and sympathetic. But she also had a job to do. She asked for Gerry's passport. I handed it to her. She took a pair of scissors and cut off one end of Gerry's passport, opened it up and stamped the inside with a big red CANCELLED stamp. Cancelled!

Gerry would have been so upset. I can still remember the day he got that passport. We were scheduled to fly to Japan for our first big trip together, and he'd forgotten to renew it. He waited until the last minute, as he always did, and then had to talk someone at the passport office into rushing the processing. "My new girlfriend will be so mad if we can't go," he'd told them. It worked. Gerry had been so proud of that passport, which bore the stamps of all the places we'd visited together. Travel had been so much a part of our lives together, and now, looking at that CANCELLED stamp, I suddenly realized we would never get the chance to see another country together.

As I arrived at the terminal in New Delhi, Alex Hanin texted me again. "I need a password," he said. "I need it to access something for Quadriga." The only password of Gerry's I actually knew was the one for his cellphone, since I'd seen him open it so often. I unlocked his phone and flashed open his Google Authenticator app. Gerry was obsessed with security; he told me he used that app to prevent hackers from sneaking onto Quadriga's websites. If someone tried to gain access, even with a correct username and password, he explained, the site would demand a second password. That second password was generated automatically by the Authenticator app, using an algorithm. But you needed to be signed into the app and have it open on your device to see that second password. To make everything even more secure, the password changed every few minutes. When I opened the app today, I noticed a number of passwords, so I made screenshots of all of them and forwarded them to Alex.

"That's the one I need," he texted back. I didn't know what for, and I didn't ask. But I was beginning to realize I was going to need to ask—because I was going to need to know. Now that Gerry was dead, I would need to step up, run the company, honour Gerry's memory. But there was still so much I didn't know about his company, what it did and how it functioned.

Thank God for Gerry's "dead man's switch." Sometime in the summer of 2017, for no real reason I can think of now—we were sitting in my office, he was drinking a glass of wine—Gerry told me that if anything ever happened to him, he'd set up a system to make sure I got an email with all the information I needed to know: passwords, details about accounts, everything. He said he'd already written the email, which was stored on a private server. Every so often—he didn't say how often—the server would automatically send him an email with a link. If he clicked on the link, the server would know he was OK and do nothing. If he didn't respond, however, the server would wait a specified period of time—again, Gerry didn't say how many hours, days or weeks—and then activate his dead man's switch, sending the email to me.

Now I just needed to wait for the switch to be activated and for everything to become clear. Nothing yet.

An Air Canada representative brought me to the business class lounge to wait for my flight. Gerry and I had always flown business class, so we were always in lounges like this one. All Gerry ever wanted to do was work on his laptop, and I would get bored and annoyed. Now I was here, all by myself, thinking how desperately I wanted to see Gerry sitting here working and be annoyed with him. I looked over and saw another couple just sitting together at a table. You don't realize how awesome normal seems until it isn't.

Nothing was normal anymore.

But I had no idea how not normal my world was about to get.

8

Where's the Money?

*W*here's the money? . . . The hot wallets? . . . Gerry's safe? . . . Did he have a safe? . . . Did you get the email he promised? . . . Who's his lawyer? You need to contact his lawyer . . . Where's the money? . . . We need the money . . . $250 million—today! . . . Was there a will? There must have been a will! . . . Where's the will? You're the executor . . . Open casket? Closed? . . . Have you got a lawyer? . . . Where's his laptop? . . . The safe isn't where you said it was! . . . What about the CIBC cheque? . . . Did you find the cold storage yet? . . . That safe in the basement? You must know the codes . . . think! . . . Where's the money? Where's the money?!

My comfortable, peaceful, satisfying world, which had been cratered by the sudden earthquake of Gerry's death barely two days earlier, was now being washed away by a massive tsunami of questions I couldn't answer and demands I wasn't ready to deal with.

Today—tomorrow? What day was it in India, anyway?—Gerry and I should have been flying from Jaipur to Hyderabad, then on to Venkatapuram by car for the official opening of the Jennifer Robertson and Gerald Cotten Home for Orphaned Children. I should have been handing out the teddy bears I'd brought, one for each of its twelve children.

Instead, Gerry was dead, his body at a funeral home in Halifax, and I was back in Fall River, overwhelmed with grief and wanting nothing more than to crawl into our bed and cry myself to sleep.

My mother and Tom had flown to Toronto to meet my overnight flight from India and then accompanied me back to Halifax on an Air Canada flight early Tuesday morning. My dad, my brother and his wife, a number of cousins, an aunt and my best friend, Aly, were all waiting for me in the airport chapel, the only large private space where we could gather. So, too, were Gerry's parents and his brother and sister-in-law. They'd flown in the night before and were staying at our house in Fall River.

Alex Hanin had already texted that he was on his way from England. "Do you have his laptop?" he demanded again. "With you?" I hadn't let it out of my sight.

Inside Kinross, I saw that Gerry's office was open, the door's lock smashed. My stepdad and my father had done that on Sunday after I called from India, desperately looking for Gerry's health card so I could give the number to the doctors in Jaipur. When we'd departed Canada for India, Gerry had left his office its usual mess—classic Gerry—and Tom and my father hadn't been able to find his health card in the jumble. Tom later told a private investigator they'd opened one desk drawer to look for the card, and "it was jammed full of papers, so much that they couldn't get the drawer closed. They left it as is." Not that they could have found the card anyway. Soon after Gerry died, I discovered it in India, in a pocket of his briefcase.

Now, on my way to our bedroom, I glanced into his office and was astounded at the number of people there—Gerry would have hated that—and how un-Gerry the room looked. Jess, Brad, Gerry's parents and Alex had cleaned his office, organizing Gerry's papers, making it seem even more un-Gerry-like. They'd probably been looking for his will.

"Where's the will?" Cheryl asked that first night after I landed in Halifax. "Did Gerry have a will?"

I didn't want to deal with that. I didn't want to confront my own feelings of guilt, either, but those wouldn't let me go. What if I'd found Gerry's health card sooner? Jess sat on my bed and reassured me. It had been a Sunday, she said again. It would have been impossible to track down Gerry's records in time, and they might not have helped anyway. *But we went to India, and Gerry didn't want to go. What if . . . ?* "Could have happened anywhere," she reassured. Gerry had been lucky. He'd been in a good hospital with a modern intensive care unit. I tried to process that.

After Alex arrived, the tension and intensity levels inside the house immediately ratcheted up. Alex was clearly panicked. "Where's the money?" he kept demanding in a thick French accent that seemed even more brusque than the words themselves. "We need money now!" To keep Quadriga operating, he told me, he needed to get access to Gerry's cryptocurrency accounts. I tried to log in, but I didn't have the correct passwords for his computer.

In retrospect, I think Alex and I—and the other contractors I'd meet later—were all stunned by the fact that none of us knew what we now desperately needed to know.

I, for one, didn't even totally understand all the jargon—hot wallets, cold wallets. I had to learn quickly. Since you can't securely keep cryptocurrency in conventional bank accounts, people use virtual "wallets" to store and protect their holdings. The wallets don't contain actual cryptocurrency, but are just tools for managing the blockchain—the official recording of what's been bought and sold. "Hot wallets" are connected to the internet and can be used by investors to buy, sell and trade cryptocurrency with other users in real time. The downside of hot wallets is that, because they're connected to the internet, they're vulnerable to hackers and assorted mischief makers. Which is where "cold wallets" enter the picture. They exist offline, often on USB sticks and CDs, so they're more secure, but that makes it more difficult and time-consuming to move them online for buying, selling and trading. It's all way more complicated than that, but that's probably all a layperson like me needed to know to understand how it all worked.

Whenever Quadriga's internet-based hot wallets were low on cash, contractors told me they would simply contact Gerry, who would magically top up the funds from an offline cold wallet so they could continue processing payments for clients. No one seemed to know where Gerry kept the cold wallets he used to replenish the hot wallets. Even if they had known that much, they still wouldn't have had a clue as to how to get into them if Gerry wasn't available. Or now that he was dead.

As surprising as that initially seemed, I quickly realized with a start that it was vintage Gerry. He was always the leader, the authoritative voice to whom others inevitably deferred. Knowledge was power, and Gerry held it all.

Alex eventually tracked down some permission forms he said

he needed me to sign as Gerry's executor. He believed they might help him get inside Gerry's locked laptop. "You have to sign these," he said. "Now."

I'd never met Alex before. I knew he'd grown up in France but now lived in the United Kingdom. Once, Gerry showed me a photo of Alex with his family, travelling somewhere in Europe. That photo was the only reason I even knew what Alex looked like. I did know he was Gerry's main web designer and programmer, and that they had been working together since the first days of Quadriga. They communicated daily. "There's no one in the world who could steal from me, except Alex," Gerry would joke. "That's why I pay him so much." He told me he paid Alex a million dollars a year.

Gerry trusted Alex. I knew I should, too. I needed his help to figure out how to cope with Gerry's business affairs, but that didn't stop me from resenting his presence. Didn't he care about Gerry? Gerry might have paid him very well, but I also believed they'd been buddies. So, why did he care so much about Quadriga and so little about Gerry? Who cared about money at such a moment? Who cared about Quadriga at all? Gerry was dead! Honestly? In that moment, I wanted to tell Alex to fuck off. It was only later, when I began to understand the full scope of the crisis Gerry's death had triggered for Quadriga, for Alex, for its investors and ultimately for me, that I finally began to comprehend why Alex had been so panicked.

Did Gerry have a safe? Alex wanted to know. Perhaps the codes he so desperately needed might be inside. Maybe there would be cash, too. Yes, I said. Gerry had installed a safe in the attic of the garage a few months earlier. "I found an awesome spot to hide my safe," he'd told me at the time.

But the safe wasn't there. Someone checked and reported back that they'd only found an indentation in the ceiling insulation where the safe had been. What the——?

There was another safe, I remembered. In the basement. Gerry told me once he had several million dollars in that safe. Brad and Alex went to look. It was locked.

"What's the passcode?" Alex demanded.

"I don't know."

"You don't know the passcode?" Alex was incredulous.

"Why would I?" I retorted, becoming more frustrated by the moment. "I didn't need the money. I never needed it. I had all the money I could possibly want. And if I ever did need money from the safe, I could just ask Gerry." Except now I couldn't. (Later, we hired a locksmith to come and blow the lock off. When he did, it turned out the safe was completely empty.)

It took everyone a while to realize that yet another safe sat on the floor in Gerry's office. Was it the one that had been in the attic of the garage? It looked like it. Had Gerry moved it there before we left for India? Left it in his office and locked the door? Or was it a different safe altogether? No matter. It was already open. But it was empty, except for a bunch of envelopes, each labelled with the name of a currency: US dollars, etc. The envelopes were empty. Perhaps Gerry had sent the cash to Quadriga customers, I thought, or maybe he took the cash so he could exchange it for rupees while we were in India. It didn't surprise me that messy Gerry might take down the safe from the attic, empty its contents and then leave the safe opened on the floor. What did surprise me as I looked around the office was that there was now no cash anywhere in his office. There'd always been loose cash everywhere.

Alex asked where else Gerry might keep cash.

There's always money in the banana stand! It had been a standing joke between Gerry and me. Gerry used to visit me in my office in the afternoons, sit on my blue lounge chair with his glass of wine while we chatted about everything and nothing. "Your chair has a big hole in it," he would say, flipping it over, pointing out a Velcro fastener that sealed a hole in its bottom. "You know, you could put a lot of money in here." As a joke, Gerry had stuffed money into the bottom of the blue lounger. "There's always money in the banana stand!" he would say, and smile and wink.

Gerry was a fan of *Arrested Development*, an American television sitcom with a cult following about a formerly wealthy California family still trying to maintain their lifestyle, even after they'd gone from "riches to rags." The show featured a running gag about a "banana stand" the family patriarch, played by Jeffrey Tambor, opened in 1953. After Tambor ends up in jail for fraud, he insists, "There's always money in the banana stand." The family assumes that simply means they'll always be able to generate revenue from selling frozen bananas, but they discover—after the banana stand burns down—that Tambor had literally hidden hundreds of thousands of dollars inside the banana stand's walls.

"Look in the chair in my office," I said. But they found no cash there, either. What had happened to it?

"WE'RE GOING to recommend a closed casket," the funeral director suggested quietly. It was now the Wednesday after Gerry's death, and we—me, my mom, my stepdad, Tom, Bruce and Cheryl, Brad and Jess—had come to the Snow Funeral Home to make final arrangements for Friday's service—flowers, music, what to serve at the reception, that kind of thing. We'd settled on a casket—stainless steel and modern, exactly the kind Gerry would have wanted. We'd talked about how we'd like him to be dressed: pyjamas! Gerry hated fancy clothes, never wore them if he could avoid it, always worked in his pyjamas. So, we would dress him in those and a huge East Coast Lifestyle sweatshirt, plus a pair of old shoes he loved. They were worn, and there were no grips on the soles, but those shoes had been his favourite. "You need new shoes," I used to kid him. "You can afford a new pair." "I don't want a new pair," he would insist. We would bury him in the shoes he loved. And, oh yes, we'd put a picture of our dogs, Nitro and Gully, in the casket with him, too. For company.

A closed casket? As delicately as possible, the funeral director explained that Gerry's body was severely swollen, partly as a result of all the efforts the doctors in India had made to save him, partly because of the handling of his body during its long journey home. Because of the swelling, he also recommended that we not shave off Gerry's nine-day growth of stubble, even though we'd explained Gerry preferred to be clean-shaven. Although he'd often grow a "vacation beard" during our trips, Gerry would shave it off as soon as we returned home. But if the funeral home had to shave his face now, we were told, there could be bumps, and the swelling would be more obvious. We agreed to the closed casket.

On the morning of the funeral, Snow's funeral director asked us if we wanted to view Gerry's body one last time before everyone else arrived. Tom and my mom said no; they wanted to remember Gerry as he'd been. The rest of us said yes. I didn't want to give up the last chance I'd ever have to see Gerry. I was first. I walked up to the casket and looked down. As we'd been warned, his face was swollen and outsized, not at all the Gerry I'd known. I turned around and walked numbly back to my chair, sat down and began to cry. I looked up and saw Bruce and Cheryl; they were hugging each other. How awful it must be to see your son like that, dead in a casket.

At the time, the decision to keep the casket closed had seemed simple, logical. But the fact it was closed would soon spawn dozens of conspiracy theories on the internet. Did he really die? Ironically, during our meeting at the funeral home that day, the funeral director showed us a pendant with a fingerprint on it. Would I like him to take Gerry's fingerprint and turn it into a similar memento? I would. I still have it, more proof that Gerry's body was inside the coffin. Not that anything I could say or show would convince the doubters. The funeral home, in fact, would soon be flooded with callers demanding to know if Gerry had really been in the coffin. According to the funeral home, someone even showed up weeks later, claiming to be from the RCMP, to ask about the casket. As my lawyer told me later, it might have been a rogue Mountie who just happened to be curious, or someone pretending to be an officer, or it could have actually been a real RCMP investigator. Whatever. It was disconcerting.

The fact that Gerry's death wasn't officially announced until January 14, 2019, more than a month after he died—and then in a Facebook post on the Quadriga page—only added an extra layer to the mystery and the questions.

The answers were always far more mundane than the rumours. Alex, for reasons I slowly came to understand, wanted to be sure there would be enough funds available to deal with any run on Quadriga's accounts once news of Gerry's death became public. The looming Christmas business break meant lining up funds— finding a bank in which to deposit the court-ordered $30 million CIBC cheque, for example, and making arrangements with Quadriga's payment processors, who had previously dealt only with Gerry, to handle withdrawals—could take even longer.

The enforced silence around Gerry's death was especially difficult for me. I desperately wanted to reach out to friends, beyond my immediate tight circle of family and closest friends, to let them know what had happened, to share my grief and feel their comfort. But everyone warned me not to. "We have to keep this quiet for now, for everyone's good."

* * *

"ARE YOU READY?" Gerry's mother asked. It was a cloudy, seasonably cool afternoon, and we stood together near Gerry's graveside at the Riverlake Community Cemetery in Wellington, a fifteen-minute drive from our house in Fall River. It was a tiny cemetery, only recently opened on a former school property. So far, there were just a few headstones to mark the first graves. When it was full, there probably wouldn't be room for more than a few dozen more bodies. I'd bought the entire back row for Gerry because I knew he wouldn't want to have other people too close to him. I know that sounds strange, but I believe now that I was probably trying to atone for whatever I must have done, or not done, in life to fail him, to allow him to have died as he did.

Gerry's casket sat on the snow-covered ground. The priest said his final few words, and then they lowered Gerry into the ground. Although Ativan had helped me survive the first days, I decided I wouldn't take any the day of his funeral because the medication makes me forget details. I wanted to remember everything about this day.

About fifty people had attended the service in the funeral home earlier that morning: mostly family and close friends, including my childhood best buddies—Aly and her husband, Kyle, as well as Anne, who'd flown in from Calgary with her infant daughter. My real estate agent, who'd sold us our house, helped me find all our rental properties and had since become a friend, attended. So did our wedding photographer. She had supplied the photo of Gerry for the funeral home. A few of Quadriga's contractors were there, too: Alex Hanin, Dwayne Siemens, Peter Huong and Aaron Matthews.

Aaron, who lived in a trailer in New Brunswick, had only been with the company for about a year. Gerry had never met him face to face and initially hired him online just to provide customer service. But he told me he'd immediately been struck by Aaron's intelligence, enthusiasm and work ethic. In fact, Gerry once said he hoped Aaron would someday take over the day-to-day running of the company so he could focus on "more innovative stuff, maybe create new companies."

Unlike Alex, Aaron was unfailingly helpful as we began to sort out Quadriga's tangled business affairs. At one point, he messaged me to tell me he'd discovered that one of Quadriga's contractors in Vancouver was holding $5 million in bank drafts intended for Gerry. The contractor apparently hadn't been able to cash the cheques and send them to Gerry because his bank, realizing the funds were bitcoin-related, closed his accounts. Gerry had known all this, but—in his Gerry way—had described it as just another "problem for future Gerry" and written it off. But Aaron arranged to collect the funds and then offered to send them to me "so you have them." My immediate response was to contact my lawyer and let him deal with it. I didn't know much yet, but I already knew enough to make sure anything done from this point on was done legally. I also knew I wanted Aaron—rather than Alex—to be in charge of Quadriga's day-to-day operations.

Meanwhile, Alex, who planned to return to England after the funeral, had asked me for every laptop Gerry owned so he could take them back with him and try to unlock their secrets. Gerry had a bunch of laptops. Whenever he upgraded, he never threw out his old ones. Old ones, new ones, I knew that I knew nothing that could help unlock any of them. I was hopeless with technology. "Why isn't my computer working?" I would ask Gerry. He'd laugh, come over, press a button and make it work. "How did you do that?" I would marvel. So, I was more than happy to give the laptops to Alex. I even tried to find the one Gerry had accidentally spilled his drink on during one of our cruises to see if he could rescue its data. No luck. But I turned over the others gladly. Let Alex figure out how to make them cough up Gerry's secrets.

At this moment, however, I didn't care about any of that. Today, we were burying the love of my life. Anything else would be a problem for future Jennifer.

"Are you ready?" Cheryl asked again.

"OK," I said, and we walked to the waiting car for the drive back to Kinross.

* * *

DO YOU remember the time when you first met Gerry?

Yeah, he picked us up in his car after . . . we were at the Madonna concert! We got in the back seat, and remember, there were candies everywhere, all over the back of the car. That was the first time I realized just how much Gerry loved his candy.

Anne, Aly and I were sitting on the floor of my living room with Aly's husband, Kyle, drinking Gerry's favourite wine and reminiscing. I was crying and laughing and crying some more. I was still wearing the black dress I'd worn for the funeral. My sister, Kim, had bought me a green scarf because green was Gerry's favourite colour, and I was wearing that, too.

We'd returned to Kinross after the gravesite ceremony. My cousin Haley made chili for everyone. But by late afternoon, almost everyone else had left, leaving just Anne and her baby girl, Aly and Kyle, Brad, Jess, Bruce, Cheryl, Tom, my mom and me in the house.

The stories poured out with the wine. About that evening, just a few nights before we left for India, when Tom and my mother had come over for a quick goodbye dinner that turned into a kitchen party. We'd dressed up in funny Christmas sweaters, and Tom taught Gerry how to play the spoons. It had been our last night all together. Now Tom brought out the spoons again. We played music Gerry loved. We danced. We celebrated his life, our love and friendship. It was the kind of night Gerry would have liked, would have wanted us to have in his honour.

At some point, I discovered that Cheryl, Bruce, Brad and Jess left the house without saying goodbye.

I messaged Jess. "Did you guys leave without even telling me?"

She texted back that they were just going out for dinner and they'd be back.

Anne didn't think so. She'd seen them packing their suitcases.

It had been a strange, difficult few days for all of us. Perhaps Cheryl and Bruce were simply trying to find a way to deal with the shock of their first-born son's death, but they seemed to me too focused on Gerry's finances.

"That's not true," Jess replied when I asked her about it. "We were just so proud of him." Looking back, I think I understand now what she was saying, but at the time, I was trying to deal with my own grief. Talking about wills and money seemed so beside the point.

In the end, that night was the last time I ever saw any of Gerry's family. Gerry's dad and I used to talk every morning on Skype, exchanging news about our days and travels, mundane topics like that. No more. I did chat briefly with Jess in January to congratulate her after she had her baby. By then, there were stories in the news about Gerry and Quadriga and missing money.

176

"Do you guys ever talk about what happened?" I asked Jess.

"No," she said. "We just talk about the baby." And that was the end of that conversation.

IN THE WEEKS following Gerry's death, after everyone else had returned to their lives, I holed up in our house, staying mostly cocooned in our bedroom, knocking myself out with sleeping pills to escape the pain and the frustration. Where was Gerry when I needed him so much?

I would write notes to him, just short, emotionally yo-yoing snippets like the one I had written the night he died, as if I might still be able to communicate directly with him. On December 18, I wrote, "Oh Booboo, where is the email you said I would get? Everyone wants something from me, and I don't have the answers. I want your email to have one more connection with you. I fucking miss you so much, baby. I just want you here."

But then, a few minutes later, I added, "I'm actually kind of annoyed with you right now, and with Alex. Can I trust him? I really wish things had been more smooth if you were to pass . . . You always thought it would all drift away and you wouldn't care because you were gone, but I'm here. And I'm dealing with this, and I don't want to be dealing with this. I just want to be with you. Your mess is mine."

Three days after that, I wrote to him again. "I'm feeling really guilty about India . . . I wish we had never gone. I miss you so terribly. Where is the email, Booboo? I just want all this business stuff to go away, so I can just focus on being with you. I'd do anything to have you back. Are you mad at me that we went to India? I'm sorry, sweetheart."

On December 28, I spent the day alone at Kinross, surrounded by fading funeral flowers and sympathy cards. For some reason, they made me angry, sad and weepy, all at the same time. I carried armloads of the flowers out of the house and tossed them into the woods beyond our backyard fence. Once, while I was returning to the house, head down, I felt a random gust of wind whistle past me, and I sensed Gerry's presence. I looked up and saw, perched perfectly on a rock in front of me, a single rose that had fallen from one of the bouquets, almost as if Gerry had left it there for me. That night, I wrote to him again. "I've been thinking a lot about what it must have felt like for you to die. Are you okay? I liked the rose. Another sign would be lovely, sweetheart . . . just to feel close to you. You are always close to me actually. Like when you kept me warm two nights ago. I know that was you."

Then, on New Year's Eve: "Oh sweetheart, I only now understand just how much stress you were under . . . I am so sorry. This must have been awful for you. No wonder you were drinking so heavily. How did you keep it together? I so wish you could have been here to see all of this resolved and to sue CIBC."

On New Year's Day, I sent two text messages, the first from me to Gerry's phone. "Happy New Year! I love you!" And then I sent a reply from his phone to mine. "Happy New Year! I love you too!" It was silly, just another way in which I tried to connect with him, another sign of how much I missed him. But later, after we'd hired a private investigator to search for Gerry's missing passwords, he came across that text message sent from Gerry's phone, which had been sent after he had died. In his preliminary report, he raised the question of what it might mean.

"That was me," I had to confess quickly. "I sent the texts. I just missed him so much."

Finally, I added a New Year's Day entry in my notes to Gerry: "Gully waits for you by the door on his chair like he used to wait for me. We all want you to come home, sweet angel. We miss you."

9

Playing for Time

I'd always assumed Gerry would not die. When he did, I assumed there were others inside his company who would know exactly which buttons to press and which codes to key in, who would be able to step in and step up to keep Quadriga running smoothly and keep its clients happy. I was wrong.

Since the courts had ordered CIBC to return the millions in Quadriga funds it had frozen the year before, I assumed the cash flow problems that had plagued the company—and Gerry—were now over. Again, I was wrong.

I replaced those incorrect assumptions with other, soon-to-be-wrong, assumptions. I assumed the dead man's switch email would magically appear in my inbox—today? Tomorrow? Next week? Next month? I hadn't abandoned that assumption, but I soon realized I needed to become more involved to try to keep the company afloat until it arrived. It was the least I could do for Gerry.

I also assumed that because Gerry and I were wealthy—yet another assumption that events would ultimately demonstrate was disastrously off base—I could leverage our assets to provide short-term funds to keep the company operating until passwords were found, vaults unlocked, frozen currency melted into liquid.

Through it all, however, I never lost my faith in Gerry. I loved him. I trusted him completely. Somehow, I was certain, even from beyond the grave, my wish-fulfilling Gerry would find a way to make those wishes—and assumptions—come true, too.

On December 19, 2018, ten days after Gerry died, Alex sent me an email from England, warning that he and other contractors had begun to wonder if they should "bail out before we sink completely." For the first time, he also put a dollar figure on what he described as the current state of Quadriga's finances. "Even with the CIBC money," he wrote, "we have a hole of more than $200 million—and that's increasing by the day as Bitcoin prices rise."

The first thing I did—after I flipped out in shock—was to contact Margaret Waddell, a Toronto lawyer who'd represented

Quadriga in its lawsuit against CIBC. Like many others involved with Quadriga, I'd never met her before Gerry died, but I thought, "Well, Gerry's smart. He would have picked a good lawyer." In fact, immediately after Gerry's death, I'd suggested Alex contact her, too. "We need help," I'd said then.

Margaret had flown to Halifax around the time of Gerry's funeral to discuss what could be done to release the $30 million the courts had ordered CIBC to return to Quadriga. The answer, it turned out, was not much. Margaret had the cheque, but Gerry was the only one who could deposit it. She'd tried various banks, but none would accept it. (Months later, the bankruptcy court finally ordered a bank to cash the cheque so it could be used to pay Quadriga's creditors.) But Margaret did more than just focus my attention on the CIBC issue. She also made it clear I needed to hire my own lawyer to take care of what were sure to be complicated issues involving Gerry's estate. She suggested Richard Niedermayer, an experienced estate lawyer at Stewart McKelvey, one of Atlantic Canada's largest corporate law firms, who would soon become my go-to lawyer.

Now I forwarded Alex's email to Margaret. "How is it possible to be $200 million in the hole in just a week?" I asked incredulously. Alex seemed to be suggesting that the CIBC money, even if we had it, would be little more than a drop in a leaky bucket, but my understanding from Gerry had always been that it was the source of all the company's financial problems. None of it made sense to me. "There is no way Gerry had that kind of money floating around," I wrote. And as much as I wanted to help, I certainly didn't have anywhere close to $200 million to lend the company. "I feel so torn and confused," I added. "Any guidance would be so appreciated."

Margaret emailed back almost immediately to reassure me that she, too, had "no idea how the business could be in a negative position," but promised she would get to the bottom of it. Later that day, she wrote back to say, "We are just off the phone with Alex. It's not as bad as his email suggested." The $200 million, she explained, was the total amount of investments Quadriga was holding for its clients. The funds existed, she said, but in cold wallets at various offsite exchanges and locations yet to be identified. Alex thought he knew where "a lot of the coins" were, but he hadn't had any luck unlocking Gerry's computers, and the exchanges refused to provide any information to him without authorization.

"Which is why the [dead man's switch] email to come from Gerry is so important," Margaret noted. "If the email doesn't show up in the next little while, then you will have to get the laptop from Alex and get it to an IT professional to break into it." She recommended Chris McBryan, a retired RCMP inspector who'd started his own private cybersecurity consulting firm. We would eventually hire him to conduct a systematic search for those cold wallets we all believed contained millions of dollars' worth of Quadriga assets.

While that eased my worst fears, I understood the company was still trapped in an immediate cash flow crisis. I was under increasing pressure—from the lawyers, from the contractors—to take Gerry's place as Quadriga's president and CEO. Although I understood the logic—I was not only the executor of his estate, but also the person who'd been closest to him in life—it was the last thing I wanted to do. I'd successfully run my own small business, but Robertson Nova's operations were relatively straightforward; Quadriga was a complex bitcoin exchange trading virtually in exotic currencies, which conventional financial institutions wanted nothing to do with, inside a Wild West trading environment. I knew nothing about how Gerry's business worked and wanted to know even less.

Still, I wanted to help. I was the executor of Gerry's estate, which included the Cessna and the *Gulliver*. I called the yacht brokerage and the flying club to inquire about selling those. And then there was his Canadian Tire bank account, which he'd told me contained $10 million.

It was Richard Niedermayer, now my estate lawyer, who immediately flapped warning flags. The first of these was the fact that Gerry's estate would have to go through probate, making everything public and delaying my ability to sell off Gerry's assets or even get access to bank accounts in his name. More importantly, Richard made clear I needed to keep my own assets separate from Quadriga's. "If you want to help Quadriga to float them for the short term," he said, "do it. But you should not be mixing your money with Quadriga's money. Don't do that."

THE STATEMENT from Gerry's Canadian Tire bank account arrived in the mail in mid-January. As recently as November, when we were drafting our wills, Gerry assured me he had $10 million sitting in the account. Quadriga desperately needed every penny of that just to stay in business. But when I looked at the balance on the statement, I did a double take. I couldn't believe my eyes. Empty safes, missing safes and now this: the account contained just $500,000. How was that possible?

I looked more carefully at the transactions. Since October, it was clear, Gerry had been transferring assets out of his personal Canadian Tire account and into Quadriga. Before he died, he'd told me CIBC had been "holding my customers' money that I've already paid out to them, so now I'm trying to float Quadriga $30 million of my own money to cover it." Some of that money must have been coming from his Canadian Tire account.

Gerry was doing his best for Quadriga's customers. At the time, I couldn't imagine there could be any other explanation.

On the morning of January 14, 2019, I spoke on the phone with the team from National Public Relations, an agency Richard had recommended we hire to help craft the official statement we would release that day to belatedly announce Gerry's death, even though we still hadn't been able to gather much information about the actual state of the company's finances. I had decided the statement should come from me. Although I had not been directly involved with Quadriga at all, except for the brief period early on when I served as one of Gerry's payment processors, I was the executor of his estate and, more importantly, his wife, now his widow. I felt I had somehow let Gerry down. I wanted to atone for whatever failures on my part—travelling to India, not finding his health card—might have led to his death. I was also so proud of Gerry, and I wanted the world to know who he had been and what he'd accomplished in his brief thirty years.

Later that day, the announcement, headed "Statement from

Jennifer Robertson, Wife and Partner of Gerald Cotten, on Behalf of QuadrigaCX," was posted on the company's website. It captured everything I believed at the time:

> It is with a heavy heart that we announce the sudden passing of Gerald Cotten, co-founder and CEO of QuadrigaCX. A visionary leader who transformed the lives of those around him, Gerry died due to complications with Crohn's disease on December 9, 2018, while travelling in India, where he was opening an orphanage to provide a home and safe refuge for children in need.
>
> Gerry cared deeply about honesty and transparency—values he lived by in both his professional and personal life. He was hardworking and passionate, with an unwavering commitment to his customers, employees, and family.
>
> Through his hard work and dedication, Gerry contributed greatly to the growth and development of the cryptocurrency industry. As an expert in digital finance, he was involved with digital payments, currency and transfers of electronic value for over a decade. In his capacity as CEO, he shared his passion and expertise

in digital finance with his management team to successfully grow QuadrigaCX into one of the largest exchange platforms for cryptocurrency in Canada. We are very proud of all that Gerry has accomplished and are confident that the leadership team at QuadrigaCX will carry on this important work in a manner consistent with Gerry's vision and values.

It is in this spirit that we announce that Aaron Matthews, the current Head of Operations, is being recommended by Gerry's Estate Executor to assume the role of interim President and CEO. Aaron has been a steadfast and positive influence on the leadership and growth of the Company. His proven leadership, coupled with his deep understanding of the industry, positions him well to carry on the important business of QuadrigaCX. We are confident in his ability to ensure continued and successful operations, as QuadrigaCX provides its customers with an easy-to-use platform that simplifies the process of buying and selling cryptocurrencies.

In the coming days and weeks, Aaron will provide further updates on the Company operations. QuadrigaCX remains committed to servicing its customers in an open, timely and transparent manner. . . . On behalf of our family and the QuadrigaCX team, we thank you for your continued support.

Sincerely,

Jennifer Robertson, Estate Executor of Gerald Cotten

I cannot tell you now just how much I wish I had not decided to be the public face of that statement. I simply didn't anticipate the vitriolic personal backlash that followed, or the frightening obsession with me that instantly gripped Quadriga's investors and the media. Truth? I'd been so consumed by my own grief and the unrelenting pressure to come up with cash to keep the company going, I hadn't given much thought to the personal feelings of Quadriga's thousands of individual investors who were, by now, frustrated and increasingly angry. The larger truth was that I was trying to help them, too, but they couldn't know that.

What customers did understand, with mounting incredulity, was that Quadriga—because the platform was set up to receive deposits on an automated basis—had continued to accept new funds into its accounts even after Gerry died. Worse, during that same time, customers had been unable to make cash or crypto withdrawals, all of which had to be processed by hand—Gerry's hand. And worst, investors were only learning now—thirty-six days after the fact—that Gerry, Quadriga's founder, president and everything else, was dead. Instead of answering their questions about the security of the funds they'd invested, my statement became a red flag to their online bull.

"You should really check out Reddit," Alex told me soon after the announcement. "People are saying really bad things about you there." I knew Gerry hated Reddit, the massive online forum of forums where people get to vote up or down on other people's posts. "People go on there and say the nastiest things," he'd told me. "If their withdrawals are one day late, they go on and complain about it."

Quadriga was now a global news story, and not in a good way. The *New York Times* reported that "frustrated investors have taken to Reddit and Twitter to discuss their investigations into the company's claims and potential lawsuits. Some questioned whether Mr. Cotten had indeed died—or whether, perhaps, he had faked his death to pull off what is known as an exit scam."

As one incredulous Reddit poster put it, "Cotten is having financial troubles at his company, so he travels to India to work on an orphanage? While suffering from Crohn's he decided to go to India? Gets married and sets up a will within a month of his 'death.' Manages to set up a plan ($100k) for his two dogs so that they're taken care of. Doesn't think to make sure the nearly $200m his exchange watches is also taken care of."

"If there is any way to figure out who the angriest people are on Reddit," Margaret wrote to Aaron soon after the announcement, "then it may make sense to get coins to them."

I'd never been on Reddit and I didn't want to start now. But it soon became impossible to avoid. "Does anyone know where you live?" Alex texted. "Because these messages are getting really, really scary."

Being linked to what had become an intriguing international mystery suddenly made me—a private person with no previous public profile—the subject of intense media scrutiny. Reporters began contacting people I went to high school with, including people I didn't know or hadn't been friends with back then, names they must have plucked out of my high school yearbook. The fact they didn't find out much of great moment only seemed to whet their appetite for more. The *Globe and Mail* reported, "Little is known about Ms. Robertson, who appears to have used three different surnames since she began buying real estate in Nova Scotia with Mr. Cotten in 2016." In the months that followed, the mere fact I had changed my last name would become the subject of much uninformed gossip, slanderous innuendo and dark online speculation, twisted, like many of the ordinary events of my real life, into puzzle pieces in a grand conspiracy masterminded by the Bitcoin Widow.

After images of our house in Fall River appeared in a CBC Television news item about Quadriga, drive-by gawkers began stopping to take photos, which they then posted online. Were they just harmless tale-tellers, or up to something more sinister—possibly, as Alex had put it, something "really, really scary"? My stepdad ended up sitting in his car near the entrance to our cul de sac, writing down the licence-plate numbers of every car that drove by.

After Gerry's death, I'd had a security system—of the kind Gerry himself didn't believe in—installed at our house. I'd always wanted one, and with Gerry gone, it seemed prudent. As the alarm company saleswoman had noted, "Just little you in this big house all by yourself?" Now, as the threats mounted, the system seemed essential.

Tom finally called the local RCMP detachment. We needed them to put a stop to the threats, he explained, so I could feel safe again. An officer did show up at my house to talk to me, but he essentially said the police could do nothing unless someone actually acted on their online menace in real life.

* * *

THE SMARTEST WAY out of the company's financial and confidence crisis, the lawyers told me, was for me, as Gerry's executor, to call an emergency shareholders' meeting and elect a new board of directors. By this point, Richard was representing me as the executor of Gerry's will, while another corporate lawyer from his firm, Maurice Chiasson, had become the lawyer of record for the company itself. Their idea was that the new board would then appoint me as chair and Aaron as interim president and CEO. With new officers in place, Quadriga might be in a legal position to accept the CIBC cheque and continue operating until Gerry's last email arrived, or until Chris McBryan, the investigator Margaret had since hired, managed to excavate Gerry's computer passwords from the Fort Knox vault of his laptop.

Although Mike Patryn had long since stopped playing any active role in Gerry's company, I discovered that he and his partner, Lovie Horner, had remained key shareholders in Quadriga Fintech Solutions, Quadriga's parent company. Gerry owned forty-three percent of the shares, Horner eleven percent and Patryn, through another company, controlled the rest. The lawyers dealt directly with Patryn and Horner, who both agreed we should go ahead with the shareholders' meeting.

But then we smacked up against a new problem: Aaron Matthews had initially agreed to take on the role of president and become a board member, but Alex had apparently dissuaded him from taking charge of a company in "free fall." It didn't help that, after I'd identified Aaron as the soon-to-be president in my own public announcement, he'd also become the focus of online vitriol. "Aaron," wrote one Reddit poster, "I Hope The Cops Kick Down Your Trailer Park Door And Arrest You In Front Of Your Trailer Trash Family So Your Kids Can See What A Fucking Loser Their Dad Is." In the end, Aaron decided he wanted nothing to do with the top job.

Because the lawyers said we needed three people to form an official board, I asked my stepdad, Tom Beazley, to step in, at least temporarily. In the month and a half since Gerry's death, Tom had become my primary confidant, even though he wasn't a blood relative. Our bond was our mutual love for Gerry. While Gerry didn't enjoy spending time with most people, Tom and Gerry could sit with a steak and a glass of wine and talk for hours about anything and everything. After Gerry died, Tom became my pillar, the person I leaned on and ran every decision past. "What do you think, Tom? What would Gerry think? What would Gerry do?" It only seemed natural to ask Tom to be on the board with me now.

The third board member was a man named Jack Martel, a former Quadriga board member who'd resigned in 2015 but whose name had been suggested to the lawyers by Mike Patryn. I'd never met Martel, either, and in fact, he played no role beyond lending his name, briefly, to the new board. Our shareholders' "meeting" was just a conference call, which I joined from our house.

The other key decision the lawyers said we—I—needed to make was whether our next step should be to apply for creditor protection or bankruptcy. We hadn't received Gerry's email and we didn't have the CIBC funds. We owed thousands of investors millions of dollars. At best, the lawyers suggested, we needed a "stalling tactic" to allow time to resolve those issues; at worst, we needed to find a way to wind up the business as quickly and painlessly as possible if we couldn't locate the money.

Because I still believed in Gerry, I opted for creditor protection, essentially "pausing" everything in place until we located the missing funds. But even as the lawyers prepared the necessary legal paperwork to file for creditor protection in the background, Quadriga issued a series of confusing statements on its website. On January 28, for example, an announcement appeared, saying the platform would be unavailable while "an upgrade is being performed on QuadrigaCX and we should be back online shortly." Later, another statement declared, "Our site is down for maintenance. . . . [We] will keep you posted as we know more." I don't know who decided to issue those announcements, but I do know that by then, all of us—me, Alex, Aaron—were supposed to be running every decision past the lawyers.

It's no wonder our official announcement, three days later, that Quadriga had submitted "an application for creditor protection in accordance with the Companies' Creditors Arrangement Act (CCAA)" was greeted not with relief, but with shock and outrage. The purpose of the application, the new lawyer-written statement claimed, was "to allow us the opportunity to address the significant financial issues that have affected our ability to serve our customers." Many investors assumed it meant Quadriga was already bankrupt. The new statement also included the first admission that we had, so far, been unsuccessful in "attempting to locate and secure our very significant cryptocurrency reserves held in cold wallets, and that are required to satisfy customer cryptocurrency balances on deposit, as well as sourcing a financial institution to accept the bank drafts that are to be transferred to us."

After that, the messages and threats got worse and more frightening.

KELOWNA! I WOULD go to Kelowna. No one in the media, it seemed, had yet figured out we had a house there. I would fly to Kelowna, hide out and escape all this craziness, at least temporarily. I emailed the company we'd leased the jet from. "How fast can I get a jet to Kelowna?"

I had already been there once since Gerry died, in January to prepare to put the house on the market as a vacation rental. I'm no longer sure what the rush was, but it felt at the time like something I urgently needed to do. Being there, however, had been more achingly painful than I'd imagined. Seeing Gerry's office just as he'd left it. The drink cart I'd bought him sitting in the den, filled with all sorts of liqueurs, untouched. I wandered into the bathroom off our master bedroom and saw the big soaker tub where Gerry liked to spend hours. Gerry loved his bath. I used to come in and sit on the edge of the tub and we would talk about . . . never again. I broke down in tears.

I remember another surreal moment during that Kelowna trip. The house featured so many large windows, anyone could easily peer into the house. Although the backlash had barely begun at that point, I was already paranoid. What if someone wanted to do me harm? I walked into the kitchen, took a sharp knife out of the drawer and crouched down on the floor, out of sight. I had only taken the knife for protection, of course, but as I held the sharp blade, I imagined how, with just a few movements, I could put an end to this insane pain in my head and in my heart. I missed Gerry desperately, wanted nothing more than to be with him again. I pressed the blade against my wrist. I needed to escape all those questions I couldn't answer, all those doubter demons screaming at me from the internet. I could end it all. Right now. But after a while—it was probably only a few seconds—I pulled the blade away from my wrist and let the knife hang loose at my side. I hadn't done what I'd briefly considered, but I had considered it, seriously. In my mind, I had crossed a line.

Back in the present, back at Kinross, I considered my options. I didn't want to return to the Kelowna house again without Gerry, but it would probably be safer than staying here in Nova Scotia, where images of our house were all over the internet. I texted my stepdad: "Tom, can you come and get me? I don't think I can stay here any longer."

My initial plan was to fly to Kelowna and stay there for a few days in the hope the storm would blow over. But Tom said I should be prepared to be there for as long as necessary. "Get everything that you can," he urged.

While Tom organized the dogs, I grabbed my bag and rushed around the house, desperately gathering up anything I thought I might need. I went down to the basement, where another safe now sat on the floor. After Gerry died, contractors renovating one of our Halifax properties discovered a big, hundred-year-old, cast-iron safe. "What do you want to do with this?" they'd asked. I'd told them to drop it off at the house because I couldn't think what else to do with it. Inside, I'd stored some gold wafers Gerry had once bought for fun, along with $75,000 in cash. The cash had come from Kelowna. Following Gerry's funeral, I'd asked my mom and my stepdad to fly to British Columbia to search our house there in case Gerry had left any large amounts of cash. They found the $75,000, but it was not nearly enough to put a dent in Quadriga's needs, so I informed my lawyer about it, as well as the gold, and stored everything in the safe to await instructions. Now I stuffed it all in my bag, along with my clothes. To anyone watching, it would have seemed like a scene from a movie in which someone is literally running for their life. Surreal, and yet all too real.

But then, real reality. The jet company called back. No one could pick me up until the next day, they said. Because I was now too frightened to stay in the house in Fall River for another night, Tom and my mother agreed I should stay with them. As we drove towards their house, I scrolled through the latest messages on my phone. And there it was. A photo from Reddit. On my screen. It felt like someone was following even the inside of my brain. "Oh my God!" I screamed.

"What is it?" Tom demanded, slamming on the car's brakes.

"They know about the Kelowna house!"

We cancelled the jet. What was the point?

* * *

CHRIS McBRYAN, the investigator Margaret's law firm hired, spent most of January in a frustrating, fruitless search for the magic words to unlock Gerry's computers and the mystery keys that could open the cold wallets inside.

"Tell me about Gerry's passwords," McBryan had asked when he first visited me at my house on December 30, 2018.

I tried. Some were simple, I explained, playing off of our dogs' names—"Nitronitro123" or "Nitrogull"—or as straightforward as "Password1." Others involved relatively simple number combinations like 4455 and 5555588888. The rest? I had no idea, I told him, other than that I believed they were complex.

McBryan tried to prompt me to come up with other potential passwords using word association. Favourite movies? *Catch Me If You Can* (which would seem a more intriguing choice as events unfolded) and *Inception*. Favourite places? Japan, Singapore, Iceland. Favourite songs? "Jane" by the Barenaked Ladies and "Moon River."

McBryan followed up with what he described in his report as "personality-based questions in order to understand Gerry and provide clues to how he would operate with his computers." For example, he wrote, "a deeply emotional or family man will use personal passwords related to his family as passwords whereas an analytical mind or goal-oriented individual will use a secure password often generated by computer or complex in nature."

In his draft report, however, McBryan had gone further, describing Gerry as a "Type D personality." According to the Harvard Medical School, Type D—the *D* stands for distressed—individuals "suffer from a high degree of emotional distress, but they consciously suppress their feelings. These worried pessimists are uncomfortable with other people and so don't get the relief that emotional closeness might bring." McBryan's shorthand for all of this was to suggest Gerry had psychopathic tendencies.

When I read that, my jaw dropped. "No!" I insisted that he take that out of his report before we turned it over to anyone else—first, because it seemed such an incredibly mean thing to say, but more importantly, because I didn't believe it. Or perhaps, I think now, because I didn't want to believe it.

As part of his investigation, McBryan also tried to trace Gerry's promise about a dead man's switch back to its source. He discovered a site—deadmansswitch.net—that allowed users to set up a notification system "exactly" as Gerry had described to me, Alex and my stepdad. The site's administrators were cooperative, but couldn't connect any of Gerry's known email addresses to any of its accounts. Another possibility, McBryan hypothesized, was that

Gerry might have used Google's Inactive Account Manager to create his own version of a dead man's switch. The problem with that was that if McBryan was able to break into Gerry's Google account, he might simply create activity that would trigger the switch to reset itself for who knew how much longer. In the end, McBryan did gain access to Gerry's Google Inactive Account Manager, but found no evidence he had ever used it to create a dead man's switch.

When none of that led anywhere, McBryan proposed what he called a "brute force attack" on Gerry's main MacBook laptop, which he'd retrieved from Alex in the UK, along with other older, less-encrypted laptops and phones.

McBryan's plan was to use a computer program to generate "random letter, symbol and number combinations to guess the password." But his own initial "low-level" attacks, which tested a number of options—eight-, nine- and ten-character passwords, all in lower case letters; eight-character combinations of upper and lower case letters and numbers; even eight-character strings of upper and lower case letters, numbers *and symbols*—all failed to breach Gerry's computer security wall, even after days of automatically entering various combinations and permutations. "Gerald Cotten used a complex password phrase," McBryan noted drily. Decoding a full twelve-character combination with all the possibilities, he added, could take up to 15,091,334 years to complete.

"The brute force technique," McBryan concluded, "will not likely be successful for years." I wasn't surprised. If Gerry had so thoroughly encrypted my computer, which contained nothing but photos and personal files, I could only imagine what he'd done with his business computers.

McBryan did discover a few odds and ends of information on Gerry's other laptops and cellphones—a few spreadsheets showing electronic funds transfers, a small wallet containing $85,000 Canadian—but none of it revealed the motherlode stash of cash we were seeking.

McBryan even hand-searched our Kinross house and grounds, using remote cameras to peer behind walls and into air-return ducts, looking for any computer passwords or keys Gerry might have physically hidden somewhere. Negative. McBryan did find a photo Gerry had taken of what looked like rafters in an unfinished section of our basement. It seemed suspicious at first, but turned out to be a photo Gerry had taken after installing a dishwasher on the floor above to make sure there were no water leaks!

McBryan also brought in a fingerprint specialist who left Gerry's office covered in black dust—I could only imagine Gerry's reaction—without definitively answering the question of what had happened there between December 9 and 11. I did know that, after I returned from India, Gerry's family, as well as Tom and Alex, had transformed Gerry's messy office into a pristine space, but I had no way of knowing whether anything important had disappeared in the process. Alex confirmed to McBryan that he had often seen images sent by Gerry, showing the chaotic state of his desk, but added that "Gerry's desk was neat and the drawer empty" when he searched it the night he arrived from England. More significantly, Alex also told McBryan he was certain there was "another USB device and isn't sure where it went." Later, I looked and looked, but I never found the mystery USB.

Still, McBryan's poking and prodding did reveal some interesting information. He discovered what could have been a security deposit key, though none of the local banks he contacted had any record of a safety deposit box in Gerry's name. He also found additional security cameras at Kinross, including one in the garage, pointing to the loft where the safe had been. But there were no video files from any of the cameras at the Kinross house during the period from Gerry's death until after I returned from India. McBryan did, however, obtain video from the cameras at our house in Kelowna, recorded when my mom and stepdad searched it after Gerry's funeral. The videos documented their search and showed that—as they'd claimed—they found just $75,000.

At one point, a frustrated McBryan texted me. He'd come across repeated references in Gerry's computer to a word and phrase he couldn't make sense of. "Do you happen to have any idea what 'Boo' and 'Booboo' refer to?"

His words crushed my heart.

"Yes," I answered after a while. "Those were our pet names for each other."

ON FEBRUARY 5, 2019, Justice Michael Wood of the Nova Scotia Supreme Court approved Quadriga's application for creditor protection, granting the company a one-month reprieve from the gathering storm of angry creditors while appointing Ernst & Young, an international accounting and financial consulting firm, to help determine where the $250 million (Canadian) the company owed its customers had disappeared. I agreed to personally lend Quadriga $300,000 to help cover the costs of the monitoring.

I had asked Richard if I needed to be present for the hearing. He said he wasn't sure, but advised me to stand by, ready to drive to the courthouse if I was called. I waited with my mother at her apartment. The day was foggy. "Whose favourite weather is foggy?" I used to ask Gerry, and then always answer my own question: "Gerry's!"

I wasn't called upon, but I didn't need to be in court to sense the ratcheting hostility directed my way. Some of it I could even understand. The fact that Gerry was a young, seemingly healthy and wildly successful entrepreneur in the exotic new world of cryptocurrency, who had died mysteriously in a far-off country just six months after marrying me—a woman who'd had three different last names!—and who had expired barely twelve days after signing a will naming me as his executor . . . all sparked a media firestorm of unconnected dots, incendiary innuendo and wild speculation. But there always seemed to be more, as the media discovered new and more random ways to fan the flames.

On the day of the hearing, for example, the Halifax *Chronicle Herald* published a story about a property trust Richard had set up for me. A Toronto lawyer I'd talked to had advised me to restructure the ownership of my real estate holdings into a trust to protect my assets in case the dead man's switch email never arrived, Quadriga went bankrupt and the properties, which had Gerry's name attached to them, somehow became entangled in the corporate fallout. The lawyer had warned me that setting up a Canadian-based trust wouldn't help if there had been fraud involved. "Not a problem," I'd answered. "There's no fraud. We just can't find the cold wallets . . . yet."

But the newspaper article put a sinister cast on what Richard had set out to accomplish. Public documents the newspaper inspected "show that within a few days at the end of January, Robertson took her deceased husband's name from the ownership of the four properties, worth a combined $1.1 million, then took out collateral mortgages on all four in favour of a trust of which she is a trustee, and finally transferred ownership of at least two of those properties to that trust."

The newspaper quoted two lawyers who suggested "the activity surrounding the property is atypical." "It's unusual," said one, "and the fact that it's happening so quickly and right now, it raises questions." Amy Castor, a freelance journalist who "focused on cryptocurrencies and financial fraud," would later add more fuel to this fire when she described me as "moving aggressively to protect her newly acquired assets."

It all sounded nefarious. But the fact is, if I'd had even an inkling there had been fraud involved, and if I wanted to protect ill-gotten assets from creditors—which I hadn't and didn't—I would have done as another lawyer suggested and moved the properties to an offshore trust far from the prying hands of Canadian authorities. The possibility that Gerry had committed fraud never even crossed my mind.

In the days after the hearing, journalists parsed my every word and deed for potential inconsistencies. The *Herald*, for example, soon found Quadriga customers who challenged the claim in my affidavit for creditor protection that "I was not involved in the business of the companies while Gerry was alive." The newspaper said it "spoke with three separate Quadriga users who provided photo evidence and screenshots that appear to be showing transfers directly from Robertson's real estate company." This wasn't quite true. Those transactions weren't from Robertson Nova *Property Management*, but from Robertson Nova Consulting, the company I'd set up in 2016 after Gerry kindly offered to pay me to send payments to Quadriga users so I could stop waitressing on the side. It was essentially a clerical task that had nothing to do with running the company. And I'd only done it for a short time; I certainly hadn't thought of it as being "involved in the business of the companies."

But the newspaper story didn't stop with those "gotcha" transactions. The story also included a disconnected but clearly suspicious fact: "According to a *Nova Scotia Royal Gazette* entry from 2017, this is around the same time Cotten's widow changed her name from Jennifer Griffith to Jennifer Robertson. Legal property documents also list her as formerly Jennifer Forgeron, but it's not clear when that name change occurred."

No wonder people were suspicious. When they discovered we also owned a yacht and an airplane, and that I was now trying to sell them, my efforts to help save the company became yet another dark twist in some complex, convoluted conspiracy. I was either conspiring with Gerry, who'd faked his own death and was in hiding in some extradition-free backwater until he could rendez-vous with me and we could live happily ever after on Quadriga's customers' hard-earned investments, or I had murdered Gerry and was the real mastermind of a different plot.

The fact that none of this made any sense seemed, in strange ways, to make sense to legions of investors, creditors, journal-ists, internet trollers, lawyers, regulators and even, eventually, the police.

Where was that damned dead man's switch email? Despite everything that had and hadn't happened since Gerry died, I con-tinued to believe in Gerry and his assurance that he would send a message from beyond the grave to answer all my questions, solve all my problems and make everything right again. My only ques-tion now was: Would it arrive in time?

10

Revenge of the Trolls

"Tick-tock, tick-tock, tick-tock." The disembodied voice at the other end of my phone line began in a singsong tone that morphed into what seemed ominously like a death threat: "Time's up." *Click.* They—whoever "they" were, and it suddenly seemed like there must be hundreds, maybe even thousands of them out there—had found me.

Facebook had been the trolls' first, and perhaps easiest, avenue to track me down. Someone must have identified me from photos of Gerry and me on my profile page—I clearly hadn't paid close enough attention to my security settings—and then used Facebook Messenger to send slanderous messages to every one of my two hundred or so Facebook friends. "Jen is a criminal," declared one sender, who claimed to have lost money investing in Quadriga. "She killed Gerry for his money." I soon began receiving puzzled messages in response from Facebook friends, including people like my ex-husband's aunt, with whom I'd otherwise lost contact. "What's going on?" everyone wanted to know. I contacted Facebook. The best it could suggest was to block the person from future posts, but, of course, that damage had already been done. And what about the next person who found out I was *that woman*?

People did find me. They tracked down my phone number, my email address. Soon, they were all over the internet. I stopped answering the phone, but did pick up one night about a month later, when I noticed Gerry's parents' number on the caller ID. I was relieved. Perhaps they were calling to ask about what was happening to me now, or to offer to help. "Hello?" I said, and then "Hello" again when no one responded. The non-conversation was posted on the internet a few days later along with a boastful message: "I got through to her!" Others began texting me using apps like WhatsApp, pretending to be Gerry's friends. "Why didn't you tell people he died?" one asked, seeming sympathetic. "We wanted to go to the funeral." After a few such messages, I realized their senders were not who they claimed to be.

I had to change my phone number, shut down all my social media accounts, even get a new email address after someone plugged my name and phone number into the Oberoi hotel's reservation history, harvested my email address and shared it online. I was terrified; my life was in my emails, and I was sure someone would soon be posting my most personal messages for the world to read.

It felt like being in a movie, but I was no longer the director of my own life story. The movie had become a horror film with me in the role of both villain and victim.

The comments were worst on platforms like Reddit, where I became known as "Dead Jen Walking" and Gerry was "Allegedly Dead Gerry."

According to someone who called himself Scamdriga, I was "a greedy gold-digging whore. Married a scam artist and knowingly [spent] money on Fendi and Prada while hard-working Canadians get nothing. Fuck you, Jen Robertson, you fat pig whore. Just die, you piece-of-shit greedy whore."

My family and friends warned me not to read what people were writing about me, but I couldn't help myself. I was like the moth being drawn to the flame and then consumed by it. I've always been eager to be liked. I've struggled my whole life, in fact, to be a "people pleaser," so it hurt in ways it shouldn't have when people, even those I didn't know and shouldn't care in the least about, not only didn't like me, but also actively appeared to hate me.

Freed from the tether of identifying themselves, people offered up all sorts of wild theories and crazier speculation. "Maybe the Bit*&^ killed him after he wrote his will," suggested N200ug. "Then she Fu(*& us all at the same time." Concluded Charles005: "It's kind of obvious the guy isn't dead and this is their exit scam that will leave Jen intact with his estate."

People were just as quick to suggest what should happen to me. I "deserved to be waterboarded for hours, then crucified." But not just me—my father as well: "Hang her dad right in front of Jen." Even my dogs! "How about you give us the location of Gerry's dogs so that we can light them on fire?"

Someone who identified himself as Charles Carmichael and claimed "my life is ruined, I lost everything" suggested hiring "a hitman on the dark web." More than a few seemed ready to do the job themselves. Georgio offered to "take one for the team" and kill me. "We need Jen's address now," he posted, adding, "I'm going to court and going to follow her home." A poster named IhateCranbrook (Cranbrook, British Columbia, being just an hour's flight from our house in Kelowna) added, "I'm gonna scout out one of [Jen's] houses soon . . . My friend is already scouting one daily. I'm gonna order some GPS tracking tiles off Amazon for any cars, boats, etc." Another poster, Raise-becka, seemed to sum up the general mood on Reddit: "Let's be honest. If Jennifer was found beheaded, all of us would be filled with joy."

I understood then—and I understand even better now—that people had lost money, some of them lots of money, and they were angry. But I hadn't knowingly had anything to do with any of that. I was just Gerry's widow. I had tried to come in to fix things after he died and, for those efforts, been targeted as someone who should be tortured and then murdered in various horrific ways.

I know some of those people were just venting, but others seemed deadly serious. Literally.

As the court hearings proliferated and the lawyers lined up—"Canada's top law firms are set to converge this Valentine's Day on a Halifax courtroom, competing for a slice of the $260 million mystery behind the QuadrigaCX cryptocurrency exchange," reported the *Toronto Star*—the judge and the other lawyers agreed to Richard's request that I be excused from attending in person because of all the threats against me. During at least one of the hearings, I was told undercover police officers had sprinkled themselves among the crowd of creditors, reporters and curiosity seekers just to keep an eye on those attending. My stepfather, who continued to serve as my eyes and ears at the courthouse, made me glad I wasn't there. He told me he'd stood outside before one hearing, watching the camera crews and spectators rushing the elevators each time a door opened, believing I might have finally arrived. When it became clear I wasn't going to show up, one of the spectators shouted, "That fucking bitch! Of course she didn't show up."

"OH, WHAT CUTE DOGS. What are their names?" It was my dogs' last bathroom break of the day, slipped in during the final hour before darkness settled over the Halifax waterfront and I became too frightened to even venture outside. After the pictures of our Kelowna house were posted online, closing off that avenue of escape, I spent a few sleepless nights at my mother's house before renting a furnished apartment on a month-to-month basis at Bishop's Landing, a condominium project beside Halifax Harbour in the city's south end.

How to answer the man now asking the question? My dogs *were* cute. His inquiry about their names was probably just polite, meaningless conversation. But the reality was that Nitro and Gully were now almost as infamous as me. Their names had been bandied about in all the news reports; they were the chihuahuas with the $100,000 trust fund. What if the man asking the questions was Georgio or any of the dozens of others online who'd threatened me with real-life harm? What if answering his question would only confirm his suspicion that he'd found his target?

At some point, I called the Halifax police, who assigned a detective to my case. He apparently contacted some of the people who'd threatened me online and issued an ultimatum of his own: his investigation would "escalate" if they made any more threats against me. After that, the number of overt online death threats decreased.

But none of it made me feel safe.

My friend Mehek, the woman I'd worked with in my first, worst job in Toronto, flew to Halifax in mid-February just to keep me company for a few days. She'd commiserated with me during my divorce from Jacob. She'd been delighted for me when I said I was flying off to visit her homeland. And she'd laughed with me when I confided to her just how much Gerry hated the idea of going to India. Now, she was here for me again. We drank wine and ate sushi, went for drives and listened to music—just normal moments in what had become an abnormal time. But then she was gone, and I was alone again.

I was spending far too much time by myself in the apartment, feeling more alone than I'd ever felt in my life, letting my nightmares invade my daytime thoughts, paying far too much attention to my online bullies, and worse, worrying that they might be right. Who was I? Who was Gerry? Was this all my fault? I'd become

more scared for my life than ever, and yet, in that same contra-
dictory moment, had begun wishing for nothing more than to be
dead. I was afraid to die, but I didn't want to live.

"Their names?" I tried to smile at the man. And I just gave him
a couple of made-up names. I'm not sure now what I called them.
I only knew I needed to get away from this potential threat and get
back inside the apartment, lock the door—checking once, twice,
three times to make sure it was really locked—and keep the outside
at bay, wishing I could do the same to the demons inside my head.

I SHOULD NOT have been surprised, I suppose, that the story of
Quadriga's missing millions—with its tantalizing tales of Gerry's
"mysterious death" spiced by my own assumed role as the sor-
ceress wife of barely a few months who'd sported three different
surnames and who'd now become the executor and sole beneficiary of his multimillion-dollar estate—would generate a media
feeding frenzy. But I was still shocked. And frightened. I was not a
public figure. My name had never appeared in a newspaper. I had
never even been interviewed by a reporter. Now everyone wanted
a piece of me.

I refused to speak to journalists, partly because I wasn't emotionally ready to talk publicly and partly because I didn't know

enough to answer questions for the record. My one attempt—the official announcement of Gerry's death—had been a nightmare, so I was happy to let Richard speak on my behalf, but only when absolutely necessary. That didn't stop the press from writing stories featuring a version of me I barely recognized.

"A Widow, a Laptop, and $190 Million: What's Going On with QuadrigaCX?" demanded a headline on a web-based publication called *Finance Magnates*, which catalogued what it suggested was a "flurry of conspiracy theories," including one that "Cotten's death was faked as a way to hide the fact that the exchange is insolvent." Faked by me? By me and Gerry conspiring together? What did they believe happened inside that ICU in the hospital in India? Did they even care?

BreakerMag, another online publication that reported on the cryptocurrency industry, weighed in with a story headlined "11 Fishy Things About the QuadrigaCX Mystery." "The more 'facts' that come to light, the fishier it smells," declared reporter Jessica Klein. Among the facts that smelled to her was that I'd changed my name in 2016—"a juicy tidbit" she claimed a Reddit user named blue_dodo had uncovered. Our recent marriage? "You read that right," Klein continued. "Cotten only got married a month before his alleged death." *Alleged?* Of course. The timing of Gerry's will? More than suspicious. Klein even connected the dots from the fact that I had an official death certificate for Gerry from Indian authorities to a scam reported the month before in the *Times of India* in which six people were arrested for "creating multiple false death certificates for people trying to claim insurance." Those incidents—to be clear, because I need to be—were totally unrelated.

The *Globe and Mail*, Canada's national newspaper, dispatched a team of journalists across the world to ferret out every scrap of information they could, "in a bid to better understand how [Gerry] died, but also to get a glimpse at how a man who carried the keys to vast sums of other people's money lived." And, of course, to paint a portrait of the mystery woman who'd lived with him.

In the first of what would be a series of major articles, published on February 8, 2019—"Crypto Chaos: From Vancouver to Halifax, Tracing the Mystery of Quadriga's Missing Millions"— the newspaper benignly described Gerry and me "settling into a seemingly quiet life in Fall River, N.S., a bedroom community just outside Halifax," where we "shared a modest two-storey house clad in cherry-coloured siding, in a relatively new development that offers residents plenty of privacy and space." But the story also hinted darkly at how Gerry changed after we got together. Gerry "seemed to drop out of touch" with associates he'd known in the cryptocurrency world in Toronto and Vancouver. They were surprised that Gerry "had gotten married, much less was living in Fall River." One supposed friend I'd never heard of claimed "he'd never heard Mr. Cotten mention Ms. Robertson."

But others fared much worse in the *Globe*'s story—and its subsequent follow-ups—than I did. Its reporters unearthed an Ontario court case that suggested Gerry's former partner, Michael Patryn, might actually be a man named Omar Dhanani, "who spent 18 months in a federal prison in the United States . . . for his role in an online identity theft ring known as the Shadowcrew." Patryn denied the connection, but three weeks later, the *Globe* published side-by-side photos of Dhanani's booking photo with a look-alike image of Patryn taken from a YouTube video. Bloomberg, the business news service, later confirmed that Dhanani and Patryn were one and the same.

Did Gerry know about Patryn's past, and if so, how much? And what did he think about it? I desperately wished I could ask him, but some still small part of me was no longer sure I wanted to know the answer.

Thanks to the posse of international journalists, Quadriga creditors and conspiracy theorists rummaging through the closets of Gerry's past, I soon began to learn all sorts of things I hadn't known, and hadn't wanted to know, about Gerald Cotten the businessman.

I learned from the *Globe*, for example, that Gerry and Patryn's business relationship dated back to 2003, to a time before bitcoins, when Patryn was twenty-one and Gerry was just fifteen (as was I). They had become involved with a website called TalkGold, which *Vanity Fair* magazine later claimed was "devoted to high-yield investment programs, or HYIPs, more commonly known as Ponzi schemes."

When Gerry died, I would have had to look up *Ponzi scheme*, a term that I now know—thanks not only to the Oxford dictionary, but also to too much life experience—is "a form of fraud in which belief in the success of a nonexistent enterprise is fostered by the payment of quick returns to the first investors from money invested by later investors." According to the magazine, Gerry had been involved in a number of similar schemes and scams before I met him; among them, he served as a payment processor for a Costa Rica–based digital currency company "used by drug cartels, human traffickers, child pornographers and Ponzis to launder money."

I tried to square the kind, benign man I had known and loved with the shady scam artist described in the media reports. I couldn't.

Everything kept getting worse. The *Globe and Mail* even tracked down what it described as the "registered office of 700964 NB

Inc. . . . part of a network of entities that helped move millions of dollars around so Quadriga could take deposits and facilitate withdrawals, sometimes in the form of physical bank drafts, for its clients." The office was actually "a rundown, vinyl-sided trailer in rural New Brunswick" the *Globe and Mail* claimed was rented to Aaron Matthews and his wife. The reporter said she had encountered a man on the trailer's porch who insisted no one by that name lived there. "He begrudgingly says his name is Jim. A short time later, he declines to answer any other questions. Visibly shaking, he demands a reporter and a photographer leave the property."

THERE WERE, to be fair, larger issues at play in all these stories. Around $250 million (Canadian)—there were so many different figures floating around during this time, even I'd lost track—had gone missing, and no one knew what had happened to it. Quadriga's customers—who numbered 115,000 by one count—were real people out real money, and they were legitimately hurting, frustrated and angry; some feared they'd lost their entire life savings.

Even if everything about Quadriga had been above board and clients' investments weren't gone, but merely "lost" inside some cold wallets whose keys were bound to turn up sooner or later in an old trunk or behind a chair, the reality was that Quadriga represented a much bigger problem for everyone involved.

In less than a decade, cryptocurrency had grown exponentially in popularity, attracting all sorts of people for all sorts of reasons. But no one in authority—no government, no oversight body, no financial institution—was prepared to take responsibility for regulating the industry or protecting consumers.

Even after Gerry died and investors began clamouring for answers, the securities commission in British Columbia, where Quadriga was originally legally registered, insisted it had no role in regulating the company despite the fact that it had barred Quadriga from selling securities because Quadriga had failed to submit audited financial statements for the year ended in March 2015—something else I didn't know when Gerry was alive. Canada's banks kept tossing the court-ordered cheque from CIBC around like a hot potato, none willing to cash it. If the regulators weren't prepared to regulate, and the banking world wasn't willing to provide financial services, what could anyone expect? The more the conventional financial world refused to have anything to do with bitcoin, the more disorderly the industry became, the more susceptible it became to manipulation.

The simple fact is that Gerry should never have been in a position to hold all the levers of a billion-dollar company with no internal or external oversight. I know that now. I didn't know it then. I didn't believe I needed to. Because it wasn't my company, it wasn't my business to worry about the fact someone else should have been minding the store.

ON FEBRUARY 15, 2019, the *Globe and Mail* followed up with yet another five-thousand-word investigation entitled "How Did Gerald Cotten Die? A Quadriga Mystery, from India to Canada and Back." As part of this story, the *Globe* reconstructed a moment-by-moment account of our final hours in India, from touchdown at the Jaipur airport at 5:15 p.m. on December 8 to my checking out of the hotel at 3:04 p.m. on December 10, on my way back to Canada with Gerry's body.

On the one hand, the newspaper reported that Indian police and medical personnel had concluded as a "certainty" that Gerry had died, and the paper itself had "reviewed hotel, hospital and embalming records that give no suggestion of anything abnormal." But at the same time, the paper pointed out that one embalmer had refused to prepare Gerry's body so that he could be flown out of India—simply because the body hadn't come directly from a hospital—and concluded enigmatically that the "details the *Globe* uncovered about his final hours only add to the enigma surrounding Mr. Cotten."

The *Globe*'s story made much of our lifestyle: Gerry was a man "with an appetite for luxury, who, together with his new wife, spent as if money was no object." In India, we had been staying as "a modern-day king and queen [in] a hotel built as a modern-day palace . . . with service worthy of monarchs." Our visit to India had been just "the latest adventure for a couple whose lives were studded with signs of affluence."

Unsurprisingly, our "whirlwind travel schedule" was trotted out as prima facie evidence not only that Gerry and I lived an excessive lifestyle, but also that we must both be guilty of . . . well, something. Reporters discovered my short-lived travel-blogging Instagram account in which I'd described myself as a "travel addict and globetrotter." "There are shots from more than a dozen countries," the *Globe* reported breathlessly, "including a market in Oman, pagodas in Myanmar and a beachfront resort in the Maldives, often with the hashtag #luxurytravel. 'Sippin' Singapore Slings on my 28th!' reads the caption next to a poolside shot posted from Dubai." Of course. Those Singapore slings.

Another *Globe* reporter travelled to Belleville and talked with neighbours of Cheryl and Bruce who reported occasional sightings of Gerry's "dark blue Lexus" in the driveway and remembered his parents "excitedly heading off to Scotland for a celebration of their son's wedding. . . . [Gerry] had an air of being successful, but he wasn't flashy, said the neighbours, all of whom declined to be named out of respect for the grieving family." As for Bruce and Cheryl, they were nowhere to be found, the reporter wrote. Their antique business, Quinte Antiques, was "shuttered. . . . When the *Globe* visited the Cottens' house on a snowy weekday morning, the driveway was un-shovelled and no one answered the door. No one had seen the Cottens in about three weeks; some said they were on vacation, but no one seemed to know where."

In Nova Scotia, a reporter interviewed the manager of the flying club where Gerry had stored his Cessna but had rarely flown it. When he did show up, she told the newspaper, "he kept to himself, making few friends." He was also behind on his rental payments at the airfield, a fact—one of many, it now seemed—I hadn't known. When the manager finally tracked Gerry down by text in late November, she said, he was apologetic. "I'm currently in Toronto about to fly to India to open an orphanage," he texted. "I've somewhat overextended myself. My apologies for any extra burden I've placed on you."

Although I hadn't known about their first exchange, the woman reached out again in December after Gerry died. I informed her that Gerry was dead, but promised I would make the necessary payment. Was I interested in selling the plane, she asked? I was. Should she keep the news of Gerry's death to herself out of respect for our privacy? I agreed.

But that wasn't the way the story appeared in the newspaper. According to her, her first question to me was "How's the orphanage going?"

"My" answer: "Gerry's dead. Promise not to tell anybody." The words seemed callous, even to me, but that's because I never said them.

The *Globe* even sent a reporter to Venkatapuram to visit the orphanage we had been on our way to open, reporting that "even the couple's act of charity has left questions—and financial pain." According to the newspaper, the $20,000 we had contributed, supposedly to build the orphanage, had been "insufficient to equip the home with doors, even to its bathroom, and leaves the man caring for the orphans in crippling debt." I was stunned. This was not at all what I'd been led to believe. I immediately contacted Angel House's CEO, who investigated and reported back that the man had lied to the reporter in hopes of winning sympathy, and perhaps additional donations, from Canadian readers.

In its story, the *Globe* also published excerpts from what I'd thought of as my personal emails. After Gerry died, I wrote to the staff at the orphanage, explaining we couldn't attend the opening because "Gerry passed away from cardiac arrest" and that I was "bringing his body home to Canada . . . I am heartbroken but trying to stay strong for him." The *Globe* published that, as well as another email I wrote later to Angel House after it sent me photos of the orphanage. "It helps me feel better knowing my husband helped these children before he died."

I certainly wasn't embarrassed or ashamed of anything I'd written, but the mere fact the newspaper seemed to have access to my emails was disconcerting and frightening. It felt like a violation.

TODAY'S MEETING with the court-appointed monitor, a serious middle-aged man named George Kinsman, had been Richard's idea. According to LinkedIn, Kinsman was a Halifax-based partner at Ernst & Young who ran their Atlantic restructuring practice and had "over twenty years providing solutions to corporate entities facing financing challenges." Which seemed to describe Quadriga to a T!

"You really should meet him," Richard had suggested. "You're someone who wears your heart on your sleeve. Once he meets you, he'll realize that you're not capable of anything criminal. Perhaps if he can put a face to the name, you can build a relationship with him."

It didn't work out that way.

Richard and I, along with company lawyer Maurice Chiasson and my stepdad, met Kinsman in a large boardroom at Stewart

McKelvey's downtown Halifax law office. The meeting itself was brief and cordial, but Kinsman clearly wasn't interested in getting to know me better. His attitude was cold; he didn't even acknowledge the reality that I had just lost my husband. On one level, I understood that. He had a job to do: finding out what had happened to the money and then recovering as much of it as possible for Quadriga's customers. But, in the weeks and months that followed, I felt like I was painted as a villain at every turn, a woman whose actions and motives were to be doubted, even though I willingly turned over every email, every text message, every electronic device, every scrap of information requested. This attitude wasn't as obvious during my only brief face-to-face meeting with Kinsman, but it would become a running theme in the avalanche of emails that followed. Even after I'd answered every question about every personal expense for the previous year, for example, the emails kept pushing. *Why did you buy this? Why did you do that?* I wanted to tell him the truth: "Because we had lots of money. Because we could." Sometimes, in his zeal, he overreached. At one point, he emailed Richard to complain about a $90,000 payment to what he called a luxury travel company in Kelowna. I had no idea what he was talking about; when I checked, the "luxury travel" company was a La-Z-Boy store that had supplied all the furniture we bought for our Kelowna home.

To make matters worse for me, Kinsman and Ernst & Young weren't the only ones looking into Quadriga. On February 8, the Ontario Securities Commission announced it would launch its own investigation into what had gone wrong. "Given the potential harm to Ontario investors, we are looking into this matter and have already been in contact with the monitor."

I would end up sitting for an interview with their investigators, too. And discovering much more I hadn't known from their eventual report.

ON MARCH 5, 2019, the lawyers all trooped back into court for a hearing on Quadriga's request for a forty-five-day extension of its creditor protection while the monitor continued to try to sort out where the money had gone.

A few days before, Ernst & Young (EY) had released its latest report, documenting its very limited success to date in recovering what it now estimated was $250 million (Canadian) in cash and cryptocurrency that Quadriga supposedly held at the time it stopped operating.

Although cast in qualifiers like "apparently" and "probably," the report did not shine a favourable light on Quadriga—or Gerry. The monitor said it found one Quadriga account in a Canadian credit union containing $245,000. The account had been frozen since 2017. EY also noted the company had been "unable to locate or provide" it with formal accounting books or financial records, and it was now trying to determine whether Quadriga had ever even filed any Canadian tax returns. Never filed taxes? I couldn't believe that. How many times had Gerry railed to me about "Trudeau's greedy government" or complained about the "millions of dollars" he'd had to pay in taxes?

EY had managed to identify six Quadriga offline cold wallets so far, but found almost nothing inside any of them. In fact, it appeared as though the bitcoin reserves that had been stored in the wallets were transferred out in April 2018. Transferred by whom? Where? Why?

"To date," the report noted, "the applicants have been unable to identify a reason why Quadriga may have stopped using the identified bitcoin cold wallets for deposits in April 2018. However, the monitor and management will continue to review the Quadriga database to obtain further information." (To make matters worse, EY reported that Quadriga had discovered more than $900,000 in cryptocurrency in one hot wallet, but had "inadvertently" transferred more than half of it into a cold wallet it could not access. I had nothing to do with that; I wasn't even informed about the problem until it was reported publicly. But, as with much that went wrong at Quadriga in the aftermath of Gerry's death, many people were quick to blame me.)

The monitor had written to ten of Quadriga's third-party payment processors, asking for any funds they were holding on the company's behalf. So far, that effort had generated a paltry $5,000. "Further relief from the court," EY suggested in bureaucratese, "may be necessary to secure funds and records from certain of the third-party processors."

EY had also contacted fourteen cryptocurrency exchanges where it believed the company—or Gerry—had opened trading accounts. The report noted that those accounts had been "artificially" created outside Quadriga's own normal process, using aliases no one could connect to an actual customer, and that these accounts were "subsequently used for trading." By Gerry? So far, only four of the exchanges had responded, and only one of those confirmed it held even "minimal cryptocurrency" on behalf of Quadriga.

The only bright spot in all of this was that the Royal Bank had finally agreed to deposit $25.3 million (Canadian) in court-held CIBC bank drafts into an account for disbursements. The problem, as far as Quadriga's customers were concerned, was how the monitor planned to disburse the initial tranche of the money. EY itself would get $200,000 and its lawyers $250,000, with another $230,000 going to Quadriga's lawyers and $17,000 set aside to pay Quadriga's remaining contractors who'd been working with the monitor. But the biggest single payout listed was a $300,000 "repayment of shareholder advances." That was to repay me for the amount I'd agreed to put up from my personal accounts to cover costs associated with the company's initial creditor protection.

The lawyers representing Quadriga's creditors weren't happy with any of it, least of all the idea I might be entitled to some of it—even though I'd voluntarily lent the money to the company in the first place. They noted that Ernst & Young had asked for more information from my lawyers as well as an agreement to freeze my assets while it reviewed any information we provided. "The repayment contemplated," explained the creditors' lawyers in a letter to the court, "is inappropriate until such time as the monitor has reviewed the requested information and satisfied itself as to the source of funds used to fund the CCAA proceeding."

In the end, none of the money I lent the company—which would eventually total $490,000, all of which I'd voluntarily provided from what I thought of at the time as my personal bank account—was ever reimbursed.

By this point, all I wanted to do was wash my hands of all of it. In preparation for the hearing, I'd had to prepare yet another affidavit on behalf of the company, explaining why we needed the extension as well as recommending the appointment of a new director I didn't know to replace Jack Martel, another board member I didn't know, who'd officially resigned just three weeks after being appointed.

My hope was that the new director, Peter Wedlake, who would also become Quadriga's chief restructuring officer, could straighten out Quadriga's tangled affairs and then sell the platform to someone—anyone—else so I could finally grieve for the man I'd loved.

According to his bio, Wedlake, a senior vice-president at Grant Thornton, a large Canadian accounting firm, did nothing but work on corporate financial restructuring, receiverships and bankruptcies. In a letter expressing his interest in the position to Maurice Chiasson, Wedlake noted he would "be supported in my role by the in-house experience and expertise that we have in the cryptocurrency area including a colleague who is a certified bitcoin professional." I was reassured, and I wasn't. Gerry had also been a bitcoin professional.

But the larger truth, as I put it in my affidavit, was that my stepdad and I "have no significant experience in the cryptocurrency industry and no experience with insolvent business. [We] don't have the expertise necessary to search for or direct the search for the cold wallets."

"She wants to cooperate," Maurice Chiasson told the judge. "She wants to be helpful, but she wants to be out of the limelight." I did. Desperately. In fact, by the time the judge agreed to grant the extension, I'd already left the country.

11

Off the Table

I felt myself swallowed whole, enveloped in the warm aqua bath of the Caribbean Sea, sinking, floating feet first, down, down, down towards the ocean floor and, finally, gliding, weightless, silent, among the teeming iridescent tropical fish just above the fluorescing coral reefs and the remains of a long-ago shipwreck. This place was magic. And not just because of what I could see around me. Because no one could find me here. No one could kill me here. No phone to ring, no email alert to ping, no one to make demands on me, no gravity to weigh me down. I was free, safe at the bottom of the ocean. I felt more at peace than at any time in the four tumultuous months since Gerry had died.

I was here because of Gerry. The last time we'd been to Aruba, the Dutch-Caribbean island off the coast of Venezuela, we'd talked about how much we wanted to learn to scuba dive. Gerry wanted to, but then his Cautious Cathy stepped in, as it sometimes did. "Well, I don't know," he said. "Scuba diving can be dangerous."

I was my usual enthusiastic self. "No," I told him, "it'll be so fun. Let's do it."

But we hadn't. And now we wouldn't. Ever. So I would do it for him. He would be with me in spirit. And he was. But eventually, I had to surface. Back to the phone calls and the emails and the never-ending demands.

I HADN'T TOLD ANYONE—beyond my immediate family and closest friends, and those few, like Richard, who needed to know— that I'd decided to spend March in Aruba. Why would I? People I didn't know and had never even met seemed desperate for scraps of information about me so that they could twist it and share it on the internet. "Oh, look at her. The merry widow. Off to Aruba for a *vacation!*"

It wasn't a vacation. My family and closest friends, who'd watched with increasing concern as I became more depressed and fragile, had encouraged me to leave Quadriga's chaos behind me for at least a while. Even Richard, my lawyer, who was planning his own March break escape to the sun, urged me to do the same. Not that either of us could escape the long reach of the relentless emails. Richard would joke that I was now his only client, and I often felt that communicating with him—and, through him, to the monitor and everyone else with an interest in Quadriga, Gerry or the estate—had become my full-time occupation, whether I was in Aruba or Canada. If Richard sent me an email and I didn't respond fast enough, he would call—*Urgent! Urgent!*

Why Aruba? When Gerry and I travelled to this most Americanized of Caribbean islands for the first time in November 2016 to celebrate the second anniversary of our first Tinder meeting, it had been an optimistic, magical time for us as a couple. We were more in love than we'd been when we met. We'd bought a house together and moved to Nova Scotia. Gerry's business was expanding rapidly and seemed poised to grow even more dramatically as bitcoin prices continued to escalate. Better, Gerry had just won that million dollars in an online bitcoin casino. And thanks to his generosity, I'd acquired the first property in what I hoped would be my new career, running my own property management company. There was much to celebrate.

One night after dinner, we walked along the sparkling blond-sand beach beside our hotel, under the twinkling stars, giddy with love and hope. At some point, I decided, for no reason and every reason, that I wanted to swim in the ocean. So I did. Fully dressed. Because I could. Gerry watched from the shore, a sweet, tender smile on his face.

"Now *this* is real life!" I shouted back towards him after I surfaced.

"You're in there with all your clothes on," Gerry marvelled.

"Yep," I replied. "Don't care."

Now, fourteen months later, Gerry was dead and I was back in Aruba, alone. I was here, in part, to escape from what had become my confusing, threatening, frightening, overwhelming reality in Halifax, but also, in part, because Aruba offered me one last opportunity to bring back the Gerry I had known and loved, the generous, thoughtful, funny guy who had died not even four months before and whom I missed terribly, and to feel close to him again in a place where we'd shared such happy memories.

Gerry was not there, but he was there, everywhere and all the time. On the flight to Aruba, I'd sat with my laptop, scrolling through happy-times photos of the two of us. I cried—trying not to, failing—shielding the computer screen from the passenger in the next seat, hoping he had never heard of Quadriga and would recognize neither the photos of Gerry nor the makeup-smeared woman in the next seat. Later, standing in the small, chaotic Queen Beatrix airport, waiting for my luggage, I could hear an impish Gerry whispering in my ear: "Whose bag will come out first?" It had been our meaningless airport competition, but now it meant something because I knew Gerry's luggage would never roll off another airport conveyor belt again.

I'd never travelled alone before. I didn't like it. Aruba was a destination for happy couples, families sharing a vacation together. One night, when I ventured out to the West Deck Beach Bar in Oranjestad for dinner, the maître d' looked past me. "I'm here by myself," I said.

"Just you, then?" he asked, as if he hadn't heard.

"Yes, just me." He seemed disappointed, or perhaps just sorry for me.

More often than not, I ate one of the three items listed on the menu in the small restaurant at the Talk of the Town, the hotel where I was staying for the month, just to avoid exactly those kinds of questions and looks. The hotel staff, who were invariably kind, knew I was a widow, but not how recently or under what circumstances. I was grateful that news about Quadriga hadn't reached the island. I told them I worked in property development and was in Aruba on business. They didn't pry.

I'd used my real name to register at the hotel and to rent a car for the month because I'd had to show ID, but for everything else—reservations at local restaurants, appointments at the hairdresser or the tattoo parlour, to book activities like scuba diving or parasailing—I became Charlotte Williams. William was Gerry's middle name, and I'd always liked the name Charlotte.

Although I assumed Aruba was safe—Gerry had once claimed it was the safest place in the world for a woman—I still worried that one of my Reddit trollers might discover where I was and come after me. Before I left Canada, I'd bought a door jammer to secure the hotel room door and a key I could turn into a small knife.

Not that I left my room all that much. Some days, I couldn't get out of bed, even to get something to eat. I couldn't concentrate long enough to read the books I'd brought with me. I even cancelled a number of scuba lessons because I couldn't face leaving the room. I just lay there, overwhelmed by the certainty that I had a black cloud hovering over me.

When I did leave the hotel, it was usually to spend still more hours alone, driving aimlessly around the tiny, seventy-square-mile island in my small, white rented car. I can't remember its make; unlike Gerry, I wasn't that interested. I'd roll down the windows (there was no air conditioning), put my phone in the cupholder, crank up the music (there was no stereo system) and play, on endless repeat, the playlist of songs I'd created that reminded me of

Gerry: "Fields of Gold" by Eva Cassidy; "Stronger than Me" and "Nothing in This World" from the *Nashville* cast album; "It Must Be Love" by Alan Jackson; "When I Look at You" by Miley Cyrus; "Afterlife" by Hailee Steinfeld; "My Heart Will Go On" by Celine Dion; and, of course, "Moon River."

Then I'd just let the heat and the wind and the music wash over me. I would drive from one side of the island to the other and back again. And repeat. It only took half an hour.

One day, I travelled up the coast to take a parasailing lesson. Like scuba diving, parasailing was another activity Gerry and I had talked about trying together, but hadn't done during our last trip to Aruba. I thought I should do it now. That was a mistake. I ended up alone, awkward, in a boat filled with couples. The only good moment came when I found myself high in the sky and was beginning to get nervous; I calmed myself by thinking of all the jokes Gerry would have cracked, making fun of my fear of heights.

Although I didn't acknowledge it at the time, my life was already in a process of transition. When Gerry and I went to Aruba the first time, we stayed at the Aruba Marriott Resort and Stellaris Casino. The five-star, 411-room, $800-a-night resort was located on postcard-perfect Palm Beach near an 18,000-square-foot casino (a favourite of ours) and Ruth's Chris Steak House (another favourite). The hotel featured its own deluxe indoor-outdoor spa and a twenty-four-hour fitness centre, as well as an Italian gelato shop and a Starbucks in the lobby.

The three-star, sixty-two-room Talk of the Town, where I was now staying, was more than adequate but small, older, more down at the heels. It was located in downtown Oranjestad, in the middle of the entertainment district, across a street from a shared beach, which meant the hotel had to make arrangements with a private beach bar to allow hotel guests to get lounge chairs for free. Instead of Italian gelato, the hotel had a small convenience store where I could buy the Red Bull I drank in hopes it would give me the energy to move. Gerry would have hated the Talk of the Town. I didn't care. I hadn't come to Aruba for the beach, the fine dining or the casinos, though I did go out one night and gambled a bit, just to feel closer to Gerry, to hear him whisper in my ear, "OK, that's it. Time to go home." I had begun to be aware, too, that my days of $800-a-night hotels might be coming to an end. But I didn't care about that, either. I'd have happily lived in a shack if I could have Gerry with me.

One day, I stopped at a local tattoo parlour. Even before I left Canada, I'd decided I was going to get a tattoo while I was in Aruba. It wasn't my first. When I was sixteen, I got a tattoo on my back. A few months before Gerry died, I'd actually begun the

JENNIFER ROBERTSON

process of getting that one removed. But this was different. I knew what I wanted and why. I had researched "tattoo parlours Aruba" on the internet and found what I thought was a professional-looking one. In real life, it was in the back room of a tiny house in a far suburb. Before Gerry died, I probably would have walked away; now I didn't care nearly as much about what might happen. I gave the man the instructions: a tattoo of a dove with a rose and the words *I'm your dove. Be brave.* I used to call Gerry "my dove," after the line about flying like a dove in the Alan Jackson song "It Must Be Love." Gerry would always joke and sing it as "I'm your dove." And, of course, Gerry always gave me roses. I didn't feel any pain as the tattooist inscribed it on my forearm. Perhaps the emotional pain I was feeling was anaesthetic enough. After I left the tattooist, I stopped at a nearby grocery store, bought the fixings for a picnic—one of Gerry's favourite activities whenever we travelled—wandered over to a nearby beach and thought about Gerry.

IN MID-MARCH, we finally got permission to look inside one of two storage units Gerry had secretly rented. I'd only discovered their existence by accident when I began opening Gerry's mail after he died. While he was alive, Gerry insisted on going to the

244

postbox to collect our mail. He'd drop off whatever was for me and take the rest back to his office. I'm not sure why he did this; I just assumed he preferred picking up the mail. I do know he would have been angry if I ever opened anything addressed to him, even accidentally. "I need my privacy," he would have said. But I didn't realize until after he died just how much mail Gerry actually received, including bills for those two storage units—one in Bedford, the town where I grew up, the other in Rexdale, a suburb west of Toronto. I hadn't known about either of them before.

According to the storage company's records, the last time Gerry was inside his Bedford unit was on the Monday of the Victoria Day holiday weekend in May 2018. The Victoria Day weekend? Brad and Jess flew to Nova Scotia to spend that weekend with us. We had fun. Each afternoon, the four of us would stop at a local supermarket to pick up supplies so that Brad, who was an excellent cook, could make dinner. We'd drink wine, have dinner, talk, and . . .

I picked up my phone and scrolled back through almost a year's worth of texts. Yes, there it was. On that Monday afternoon, Gerry drove Brad and Jess to the airport to catch their flight home. I'd gone to the grocery store. "Miss you guys!" I texted Jess. "I'm solo in the grocery store." Did Gerry stop off at the storage unit on his way home that day?

By the time Richard got the OK for me, as executor, to enter the unit, I was in Aruba. One of the paralegals from Richard's office and my stepdad went to the Bedford unit. While Tom documented it all in a Facetime live video to me in Aruba, the manager of the storage company cut the lock and Tom entered. The cavernous $200-a-month storage unit was empty except for one large navy blue Tupperware bin sitting on the floor in the middle of the space. After one of them lifted the lid, Tom pointed the camera inside. The entire contents of the bin consisted of two packages of Pokémon trading cards, a thousand stamps and an undated shopping list of Christmas presents Gerry was apparently planning to buy for me. But why? I didn't—still don't—have a clue.

I had no better explanation of what we found when I flew to Toronto with my mom and Tom in June to open the Rexdale unit. Unlike the Nova Scotia storage, this one was filled with a random collection of seemingly unrelated items—dozens of Visa credit card applications in the names of Gerry and his former girlfriend, an expired passport, a video recorder, an object that looked like a book but sounded like coins when you shook it and an old backpack. Inside the backpack, we found $35,000 in cash. Why would Gerry have put it there? Why did he leave it there? Questions for which there would now never be answers.

I hadn't entirely stopped believing that Gerry's dead man's

switch email would arrive, but the more time that went by with-out it appearing, the less likely it seemed it ever would. But why would Gerry have told not only me, but also Tom and Alex that he'd set up such an alert if he hadn't? It wasn't as if any of us had asked him to do it, or even understood why he felt the need. Why would he claim he had done such a thing and not follow through?

Perhaps, I thought—hoped—the switch simply hadn't been set to trigger as quickly as we'd assumed. Three months? Three months would still be a logical time frame. If that was the case, Gerry's email would arrive sometime around the middle of March, while I was in Aruba. I opened my email every morning, scanning my inbox for the message that contained the answers to everyone's questions. Nothing. Could it have been four months? Or six? A year? Perhaps something had gone wrong. Maybe Gerry made an error in setting it up, or maybe some flaw in the dead man's switch software prevented it from triggering. Or per-haps he had sent it—and it went, as Alex had suggested it might, to Gerry's parents. We hadn't spoken since Gerry's death, and I had no idea if Ernst & Young had contacted them.

I still found it difficult—though no longer impossible—to believe Gerry might have intentionally done something wrong. Still, I resisted allowing myself to go there. The truth was that I still loved Gerry. Part of me felt as though our life together had been a dream, the best dream you could ever imagine, and now it was time to wake up. But to what? I spent a lot of time thinking, sifting, shuffling, trying to work things out in my head that never worked out. I often wished I'd died instead of Gerry. If I'd died and Gerry was still alive, he'd have known where to find the keys to open the wallets. He'd have been able to explain where the money was and make everything OK again.

I couldn't give up on Gerry by even acknowledging what so many others were now concluding about him. He wasn't around to defend himself. Whenever I thought about all the awful things people were now saying about him—which, I reminded myself, amounted only to rumours and speculation—I also reminded myself people were spreading all sorts of rumours and speculation about me, and I knew they weren't true. So, why should I believe what people were saying about Gerry?

And yet, I could be angry with Gerry, too. It was complicated. I was conflicted and confused. I missed Gerry so badly. I just wanted to see him again for ten minutes, to hold him and be held by him. But then there were other times, more and more frequent as time went on, when all I wanted was to have him sitting in front of me for those same ten minutes so I could demand answers to all the questions I still couldn't answer. "What the hell really happened?" And hear his answers.

I almost believed Gerry would still come up with a reason-able, logical explanation that accounted for everything and made everyone's doubts disappear. I wanted so desperately to be able to call up Richard and say, "See? That's what happened. Go tell them."

But I couldn't talk to Gerry, couldn't ask him. And the questions and doubts grew.

MY PHONE RANG. It was late March. I was sitting under the shade of a tree by the hotel pool, trying not to think. The sun was help-ing my state of mind. So was the fact that no one had found me, even after all this time. I finally felt my body beginning to uncoil, become slightly less tense, my mind less depressed.

Richard understood that my future mental health depended on putting Quadriga in my rear-view mirror. He had suggested approaching George Kinsman with a settlement proposal that would allow me to extricate myself from the mire that Quadriga had become, keep what was mine and get on with making a life for myself again. At the time, I was holding close to $12 million in properties, cash and other assets on my own behalf and as Gerry's executor. We already knew the monitor believed some of those assets might rightly belong to Quadriga. So, we proposed that I

would keep $5 million, mostly the Robertson Nova rental proper-
ties and Kinross, while turning over everything else, including the
Kelowna house, to the monitor and giving up any future interest
in Quadriga, including whatever the platform might ultimately
sell for. We thought it was a generous offer.

Richard had agreed to work out the details. Now he was on the
phone again with what I assumed was an update on the negotiations. It wasn't.

"That settlement," he said simply. "It isn't going to happen."

EY's investigation, Richard explained, had now concluded
that Quadriga's investors' money wasn't just missing. It had been
stolen. By Gerry. He'd set up fake accounts using fake names like
See-Threepio and Artoo-Deetoo, filled the accounts with fake
cryptocurrency and then used that to make real trades, gambling
that the value of crypto would increase and he would make money.
It didn't. Instead, the value fell, and kept falling. Gerry had lost
at least $100 million that EY been able to trace so far. Another
$80 million remained unaccounted for. Worse, Gerry had mixed
Quadriga's income with his own, using funds that belonged to
Quadriga investors to finance his lifestyle.

Our lifestyle! *Our* lives!

"There has to be something they don't understand," I insisted
to Richard. "I mean, this is bitcoin. They just don't understand

bitcoin. *I* don't understand bitcoin. And Gerry was great at making trades. He did day trades, Questrade. He made money all the time." I was babbling. "See-Threepio? Gerry wasn't even a hard-core *Star Wars* fan. Why would he? . . . I mean, Gerry loved to gamble. It's true. We would go to the casinos whenever we travelled and we had fun, but Gerry was always the one who said, 'We've spent enough. Let's go home.'" I was almost pleading now. "There has to be a mistake. Gerry's so smart. If he hadn't died, he could have explained—"

Richard cut me off calmly. "It doesn't really matter," he replied, "because Gerry's not here. If he hadn't died, maybe none of this would have happened. But he did die, and he left nothing—no instructions, nothing. So, now it's all a matter for interpretation. And the monitor has decided this is the only interpretation that makes sense."

I got off the phone and sat by the pool by myself for I don't know how long, just trying to fit together all those puzzle pieces I hadn't been able—or willing—to put into their logical places until now. The safes with nothing in them . . . the Canadian Tire bank account drained of most of its cash . . . the empty cold wallets . . . the dead man's switch email that never arrived. I was no longer in denial that all the money the monitor claimed was missing really was. But how had it disappeared? I still couldn't understand—or accept—how that had happened. And, more importantly, why? That was the part I didn't understand.

All I knew was that I felt empty, drained. How much worse could it get? And then, in the middle of all of that, I thought of how much I missed Gerry, how much I needed him now.

THE MONITOR'S OFFER, which arrived as I was preparing to return to Canada, was not an offer at all. EY had decided it was time to shift Quadriga from creditor protection to bankruptcy proceedings. "Given the present circumstances," it understated in its fourth report to the court in early April, "the possibility that Quadriga will restructure and emerge from CCAA protection appears remote."

Bankruptcy would reduce costs for the company, so there would be more to distribute among Quadriga's thousands of creditors. EY could now move on from its monitoring role to become Quadriga's trustee in bankruptcy. Since the company was not going to be restructured in order to be sold, but simply put out of its corporate misery, Quadriga would no longer need a restructuring officer or other corporate directors. Tom and I were both relieved beyond words to be freed from that burden. There was also no need to replace Maurice Chiasson as Quadriga's lawyer; he'd resigned after creditors expressed concerns that having Stewart McKelvey lawyers representing both the estate and the company constituted a conflict.

The larger question, however, was how much of Quadriga's missing funds EY could recover. Quadriga had 76,319 registered creditors, virtually all of them clients, who collectively claimed they were owed $214.6 million (Canadian). So far, EY had only recovered $32 million, much of it consisting of the formerly frozen CIBC funds. It was tracking another million or so in the hands of uncooperative third-party payment processors, and the move to bankruptcy would give the trustee the "right to compel production of documents and seek examination of relevant parties under oath."

The only other source of Quadriga funds ripe for recovery, the monitor suggested, were those assets I had believed were legitimately mine. "During the course of the monitor's investigation into Quadriga's business and affairs, the monitor became aware of occurrences where the corporate and personal boundaries between Quadriga and its founder Gerald Cotten were not formally maintained, and it appeared to the monitor that Quadriga funds may have been used to acquire assets held outside the corporate entity." EY wanted me to agree, voluntarily, to what is known as an asset preservation order so that it could do its work "without concern that assets possibly recoverable for the applicants' stakeholders may be dissipated."

I had no intention of parting with any of those assets. When I initially tried to sell the plane and the boat after Gerry died, my only purpose was to provide emergency funds to keep Quadriga operating until the cold wallets could be located. When I transferred my real estate into a trust, it was at my lawyer's urging in order to protect what we then genuinely believed were my assets from getting tangled up in Quadriga's messy business affairs.

But it was as if EY and George Kinsman had already decided I was guilty and plotting the kind of escape my internet trolls had only imagined. And if I didn't immediately agree to the asset preservation proposal—under which EY would allow me to continue to operate Robertson Nova under its supervision and earn a living, so long as I didn't try to sell any properties or move their ownership beyond the court's jurisdiction—EY would immediately escalate matters and ask the court for something called a Mareva injunction, an "extraordinary" remedy that, I understood, would freeze all my assets and put my life under EY's complete control.

Choose!

I couldn't. Not that fast, and not under such pressure. "I need a second opinion," I told Richard, and I contacted a lawyer I'd met in British Columbia. After discussing the offer with Richard, however, he also agreed asset preservation was my best—only—option. So I agreed.

But because I was still in Aruba, I hadn't signed anything. That made the lawyer for the trustee extremely nervous. Since she had had no right or need to know where I was—we'd continued to conduct business as usual via email all month—Richard hadn't disclosed my whereabouts to her or Kinsman. Now he felt he had no choice. Richard explained that I was in Aruba and would sign the documents as soon as I returned. *Aruba!* The trustee's lawyer fired back an urgent message to Richard. *Is she planning not to return to Canada?*

I wanted to laugh. I felt like crying. Why would I flee? I'd done nothing wrong. I'd tried to do everything right. How did I end up presumed guilty?

12

Good People . . . Bad Things

I'm walking through a forest when I spot him. Ahead. In a clearing. Gerry! It's really him! "You're alive," I marvel.

"Of course I am," he answers with his best silly-boy grin. "What did you expect?"

And then . . . I'm walking into a Winners department store, or maybe it's a supermarket, or just some big store with lots of customers all milling about. I stand with a microphone next to a loudspeaker, in the middle of everyone, shouting, "Listen, people. This is Jennifer Robertson speaking. I just want you to know that Gerry Cotten is alive!"

And then I'm back in India, back in the hospital, back in the ICU, back on the day the end began, seeing Gerry's heartbeat on the monitor in front of me. The doctor is speaking, but it's garbled or in another language, and I can't understand a word he says. Then the doctor disappears and a horde of faceless people replace him, surrounding me, crowding me, screaming into my own face. *You have to get Gerry out of here. Now! Now!* I'm searching and searching, but I can't find his health card. Where is his freaking health card?! And then . . . silence. The faceless shouters fade. The monitor no longer beeps. The line on the screen runs flat to nowhere . . .

I WOKE UP again, sweating, wishing I was still asleep. Reality inevitably felt worse even than my nightmares.

On this morning—Monday, April 15, 2019—I got up, walked to Gerry's office and opened his closet door. Always Generous Gerry had given me the walk-in closet in our master bedroom. He kept his own clothes in this smaller closet in his office. They were hanging there now. I leaned in, wrapped a bunch of his sweaters in my arms, smelled his smell, hugged them close as if Gerry might still be inside and willed him to be there. I heard myself sobbing. How long had I been crying? I couldn't remember. When did I start? Would the tears ever stop? The pain felt physical, and it came in waves—sadness, grief, loneliness, hopelessness—stabbing me in a million places, running over and through whatever defences I once thought I had. I couldn't go on like this, couldn't go on at all. Why would I even want to?

But I was angry, too. Gerry was dead, and he'd betrayed me, leaving me to deal with his mess. I was soon going to lose everything I'd believed was mine, including the house in which I lived and the business that had given me the job I'd loved. "It's not looking good for you," my lawyer had said. Not looking good for *me*! I muddled my anger at Gerry with all those other emotions. How was any of this my fault? What had I done to deserve the loss of my privacy, my security, even my sense of self?

But then I was suddenly sad in the middle of being angry. I still loved Gerry Cotten. I did. I couldn't explain it. And that frustrated and confused me even more. I shouldn't still love him. That must be my fault, too.

I'd been pinballing all those conflicted feelings around in my head for weeks, considering my options, and now, finally, I understood what I must do. I had planned it out in my head in advance, so I didn't have to think. I only had to act, an automaton on autopilot.

I sat down at the kitchen table and wrote a note to my parents. I wanted them to know this wasn't their fault; there was nothing they could have done. I just needed to be with Gerry, I told them. But I also wanted—needed—them to know something else I shouldn't have to say, but also knew I needed to: "If you ever doubt, or anything ever comes out and you have to question everything like I had to question Gerry," I explained, "I want to let you know from the bottom of my heart that I knew nothing of what was going on."

After I got dressed, I got in my Jeep, drove to the liquor store in the Fall River Mall and bought two bottles of Goats Do Roam, the South African white wine that had become Gerry's and my favourite. Then I drove to the nearby cemetery where, almost exactly four months before, I'd put Gerry in the ground.

I stood at his graveside and reread the words I'd written for his gravestone epitaph: *If love could have saved you, you would have lived forever.* On that day, it had all seemed so unbearably tragic, but also uncomplicatedly so. Now I stared for a long moment back at the headstone, at the etched-in image below the name COTTEN. It depicted the *Gulliver*, the yacht Gerry had been so proud of, sailing towards the sun as two gulls circled in the sky above. Near the bottom left of the headstone, another image had been carved into the black granite, this time in the shape of a heart. Inside it was a photo of Gerry with his arm around me. It was his favourite of all the photos we'd had taken for our engagement. Gerry had been so patient as the photographer kept instructing him to turn this way and that; I counted myself lucky to be marrying such a gentleman. Today, I opened one of the bottles and emptied it over the ground above Gerry's body. "I'm in so much pain," I whispered to him. "I can't be without you." With my fingers, I then carefully traced each letter of the words that had changed everything for me.

GERALD WILLIAM COTTEN

MAY 11, 1988–DEC. 9, 2018

MARRIED OCT. 8, 2018

JENNIFER ROBERTSON

I rubbed my fingers along the space below my name. Soon, my dates would be here, too.

Back at home, I gathered my pharmacy's worth of prescription medications, crawled back into bed, opened the second bottle of Goats Do Roam, poured a first glass, hit play on my Aruba play-list of all the songs that reminded me of Gerry and leafed once again through the pages of our wedding photo album. Gerry had never seen it. The photographer had only finished producing it the week Gerry died. "Oh my God," she'd said to Tanya. "Should I even tell her it's ready?" Thankfully, she had, and I'd spent many nights since turning its pages, smiling at a moment here, a gesture there, remembering that day a lifetime ago when my world was a very different place. I did so again now, reminiscing not just about the wedding itself, but also all that it had represented of our lives together and the future that now could never be.

"All right," I said to myself after a while. It was time. As I drank the wine, I also began swallowing the Ativan tablets I'd been saving for exactly this purpose. I'd read on the internet that if you took enough Ativan mixed with alcohol, your brain or lungs would slow down so much, you'd just stop breathing and you'd die. I swallowed one pill after the other, as quickly as I could. I thought I knew how much I needed to take so the pills would do the job I wanted them to do. I was determined, deliberate. I swallowed another, and another, and another. And then, nothing.

TWO WEEKS EARLIER, when I left Aruba, I didn't fly immediately back to Halifax. I stopped in Fredericton, New Brunswick, to meet with a woman named Michelle Russell. My assistant, Tanya, used to work with her. "I really think you should meet her," Tanya said. According to Michelle's website, her earliest memories, from when she was just three, were of "seeing her own loved ones on the Otherside," as she called it. She'd experienced "tragic grief and loss at a very young age" and had resolved to use her gift to help others. She'd become an internationally known psychic medium. She claimed she often worked with the military and law enforcement on cases, including one in which she'd helped the nearby Moncton police force solve a missing persons case.

Michelle claimed to receive "strong insights, feelings and images" from those who were no longer present, knew the kind of details—names, dates, memories, even body language—she shouldn't have been able to know and which her clients "unquestionably recognize as their loved ones." Her personal mission, she said, was "to inspire and reunite as many people as possible with their loved ones on the Otherside."

I wasn't sure what I thought about the idea of consulting a psychic, even as I did it. I'm not an atheist; I believe there must be something beyond the life we live on Earth. Gerry and I used to argue about it. "There's nothing," he would insist. "You die, you die."

And I would counter, "No, Gerry, I don't know what it is, but there's got to be something after you die."

"No, no," he would insist. And so it would go. Just a friendly argument between lovers. But after Gerry died, all I could think was *I really hope you're wrong and I'm right.*

Why not talk to a psychic? What did I have to lose? If she was able to communicate with Gerry, and I was able to talk to him, to ask him all those questions still percolating in my mind . . .

The stopover in Fredericton did not begin auspiciously. The plane landed at the small airport in the middle of a huge early April snowstorm. I had to lug my heavy suitcase to the rental car lot through deep snow, crying and cursing Gerry: "You were always here to carry my fricking suitcase!" I complained. "Where are you now?"

I know some people believe psychics pick up on things you tell them and then use that to make you believe they know more than they do. I was careful not to tell Michelle anything about what had happened to Gerry and me. She did say she never read the newspapers, although our story would have been hard for anyone but a hermit to miss. What she did say, though, was that she knew there were "a lot of issues" and she "sensed a lot of media attention" about Gerry.

I wasn't convinced by that, but then, when she tried to channel him, she said some things that seemed very Gerry-like. "He wants you to know he had a plan."

That was so Gerry, I thought. But it could have been other people, too.

Later, I asked her to ask Gerry what I should do about his parents. "He's saying, 'Nothing,'" she said after a while. "Don't even bother with them." She couldn't have known I'd had this falling-out with Gerry's parents or that, after our wedding in Scotland, Gerry himself said he wanted nothing more to do with them.

But in the end, I didn't get the answers I was looking for. She did say Gerry had told her he'd had a plan, that he'd taken "money" out of the "bank" because he thought it would be safer if he stored it in his "house," but then the house "burned down" unexpectedly and he had nothing. According to Michelle, this was metaphorical. Gerry was explaining that he'd moved something valuable from a conventionally secure place into some place not so conventionally secure, thinking it would be safer, but then a disaster happened "and it all disappeared."

None of that answered my real questions: *Where's the money, Gerry?* and *Why? Why?*

Driving back to Halifax in the snow in the rental car, other questions swirled like snow inside my head. *What am I going to do now? What's going to happen to me?*

No one, in the present or from the Otherside, answered me.

As USUAL, my older brother was there for me when I arrived home from Fredericton. It wasn't as though Adam and I talked every day, or even every month, but when things were really good—or really, really awful—he was always there for me. When Jacob asked for a divorce, for example, Adam was the first one who called me. He bought me an airplane ticket so I could come home from Toronto, and he met me at the airport. Four years later, when I returned from India with Gerry's body, Adam was there again, among those waiting at the airport for me.

On this day, we sat in my kitchen and he just listened while I gave vent to all my doubts about everything I'd done and not done. "I don't know why I didn't ask for an autopsy," I said at one point.

He gave me a look. "Why would you?" he asked simply.

He was right. There had been no reason for me to ask for an autopsy. I had seen Gerry die. I'd talked to the doctors. I knew about his Crohn's. And yet, I had begun to let everyone else's opinions twist my thinking, making me question even those facts I knew to be true. This couldn't go on.

WHILE GERRY WAS ALIVE, I was a financially independent woman. In part, I knew this was because I was the beneficiary of what I'd believed at the time was the honestly earned product of Gerry's business success. But it was also because of the person I am. From my first Tim Hortons job when I was sixteen, I'd been determined to pay my own way. My failed marriage, and the financial price I paid when it ended, had made me even more conscious of my need to be in control of my own financial destiny.

Gerry was the first man I'd ever been with who earned more than I did. When I moved in with him and Gerry offered to cover the monthly condo bills because he already was paying them anyway, I was nervous about accepting. I didn't want to be dependent. I only finally gave up my part-time bartending and waitressing gigs when Gerry offered to pay me to process Quadriga payments. He paid me like any other contractor performing the same necessary job for him, the bonus being that I didn't have to be on my feet at a bar all night. After I lost my job with Travelers in the fall of 2016, my immediate plan was to look for another HR job so I could continue earning my own income, even though it was clear by then I didn't need to work if I didn't want to. But Gerry offered me a better opportunity: launching my own property management firm, seeded with cash he'd won in a bitcoin casino. Did Gerry really win a million dollars in a bitcoin casino, or was that just money he stole from Quadriga's customers? I don't know anymore. I did see the deposit slip, but I don't recall the details written there. I also know he later told me that the casino had shuttered its doors. At the time, of course, I had no reason to question his—and my—good fortune.

That fortunate beginning notwithstanding, I'd worked hard to grow the business—*my* business—which now seemed like it was about to be taken away from me, making me one more victim of whatever it was that Gerry had done that I did not know about or still fully comprehend.

I still didn't know how he'd done what he'd done. Or why. I only knew I'd done nothing wrong. I'd cooperated with the monitor, and then the trustee, at every turn. I'd handed over Gerry's computers and his cellphone containing all our most personal texts. I didn't delete anything, didn't hide anything, answered every question I was asked, even the worst: *Is Gerry really dead?* Despite that, I was made to feel like a criminal, and not just by those on the internet. I was being asked to sign all sorts of documents, agree to all manner of restrictions on my life. The "voluntary" asset preservation order—the details of which would soon be made public, making me seem even more guilty—froze all of my assets, even those unconnected to Gerry or Quadriga, limited how much I could earn from Robertson Nova Property Management, restricted me to one credit card, checked every purchase I made and allowed the trustee to monitor all my bank accounts and approve every transaction.

It wasn't so much the restrictions themselves that bothered me, but the judgment of me that came with them: that I was a bad person, a person who could not be trusted. Nothing would ever be as awful as Gerry dying, but those days in the first weeks of April, while the details of the asset protection order were worked out and I found myself the villain in someone else's story of my life, came close.

Even my lawyer seemed to doubt me. I know now, in my reflective moments, that Richard—like George Kinsman—was just doing his job, performing his due diligence, but it sure didn't feel like it at the time. "So, I just want to know for sure," Richard would say too many times. "You really didn't know anything, right?"

ON APRIL 8, 2019—yet another date with an eight, now a bad omen in my life—Justice Michael Wood of the Nova Scotia Supreme Court acknowledged the inevitable: there was no hope of restructuring Quadriga. The company officially entered bankruptcy proceedings. At the same time, he granted Ernst & Young's request for the asset protection order. Reported the Canadian Press, "The order applies to all assets held by Cotten's widow, Jennifer Robertson, and the Cotten estate, including some of Robertson's trusts and businesses. The order prohibits Robertson from selling, removing or transferring any assets. However, it allows her to cover her legal and living expenses by granting her access to two bank accounts overseen by Ernst and Young." Not charged. But guilty anyway.

"A CRYPTO MILLIONAIRE, Loose Ends and a Dead End," read the headline above the story in the April 10 edition of the *Economic Times of India*. Four months after Gerry died, the global media remained fascinated with Quadriga, fixated on Gerry, on the still-missing millions and on me, his "bitcoin widow."

Much of this story was yet another rehash of already published fact, fiction and speculation—my change of name, Michael Patryn's changing identity, the timing of the will, Gerry's "alleged" death, the medical college's unwillingness to embalm the body, even the hotel's refusal to say more than it had already said so often. Which made everything seem even sketchier. "We have already made our position clear," the Oberoi Rajvilas said in what appeared to be a well-worn statement. "All the information is out in the public domain."

Stephen Chittababu, an administrator for Angel House India in Hyderabad, did his best to downplay the controversy—"Gerald died in his prime. God bless his soul"—but the paper couldn't resist fanning the flames: "Or did he?" began its next paragraph, requoting that earlier *New York Times* article that suggested Gerry might have faked his death "to pull off a grand exit scam."

But I also discovered some new information in the article about the orphanage in Venkatapuram, which Gerry and I were supposed to open. The article described the orphanage, which I'd never actually seen, as a single-storey, olive green–walled home on elevated ground, its facade featuring "a plaque with the names of the two patrons." Inscribed beneath were the words of encouragement I'd written: *Follow your dreams. Reach for the stars. Let your heart be your guide.* I won't pretend the words are profound, but I'd wanted something simple and easy for the children to understand, something that would motivate them each day.

It also turned out that the teddy bears I'd brought to India for the children and asked the hotel to send on to the orphanage had still not arrived. The story suggested they were "probably hibernating somewhere in a five-star luxury hotel in Jaipur—or they are simply lost in transit."

Pastor Cherukupalli Rama Rao, who ran the orphanage with his wife, told the reporter I had reached out to him in June 2018 to ask about supporting the children through Angel House. Not true. I'd only ever spoken to officials at Angel House in the US. Rama Rao also told the reporter that not all of the promised money had arrived. Although he'd been able to buy most of the necessary construction materials for the orphanage, he said, "he had to dip into his personal finances to provide basic necessities for the children."

When I'd contacted Angel House after something similar appeared in a *Globe and Mail* story, an official insisted it was simply Rama Rao's way of trying to wheedle donations from the newspaper's readers. I no longer knew what to believe. I only knew I desperately wanted to make it right. In another time, not that long ago, I could have done exactly that. I could have got on a plane and flown to India. Made sure the orphans had whatever they needed. No longer. There were so many things I could no longer do. My life was spinning out of control in more ways than one.

I DON'T KNOW now how long I was unconscious after I swallowed the pills and the wine. When I looked over at the clock on the bedside table, it said 6 a.m. I was groggy and confused. Where was I? What had I done? I could feel the pressure of the wedding album on the bed underneath me, poking up against my body. Was I alive, or . . . ?

I tried to get out of bed. Everything seemed gauzy, out of focus, and I stumbled around, barely able to put one foot in front of the other. I couldn't think, couldn't function. At some point, I picked up my cellphone and pressed numbers on the keypad: 9-1-1. I didn't intend to. I was supposed to be dead; I wanted to be dead. But I was alive, and in spite of myself, I was now calling for help. I don't remember what I told the person at the other end of the line; I do know, because I was told later, that it took the ambulance half an hour to arrive because the emergency service was so busy that day, and that I talked to the operator while I waited. I have no clue what I said to her.

By the time the ambulance arrived at the Queen Elizabeth II Health Sciences Centre in Halifax, my mind had cleared enough for me to understand I had tried to kill myself, failed, and then inexplicably reached out for help. I was . . . embarrassed. And angry with myself for failing to accomplish what I had set out to do. I ended up in a hallway in the ER on a gurney while they tried to find a bed for me. When I realized no one was paying attention, I decided to try to finish the job before it was too late. I grabbed some of the wires and tubes I was hooked up to, wrapped them around my throat and tried to choke myself. It makes no sense even to me now, but that's what I did. A paramedic quickly grabbed my hands to stop me. I fought back, but he won. I gave up and disappeared again into my Ativan haze.

"Who do you want us to call?" a nurse asked at some point.

"My assistant," I said. "Call Tanya." It wasn't fair to her, but I knew I couldn't face my family at that point. Truth? I still haven't told my parents about my suicide attempt. I'd never been able to talk to my father about personal stuff. And my mother, who'd had her own mental health issues since I was a kid, had begun spiralling deeper into her own anxiety, paranoia and OCD even before Gerry died. When we travelled with my mom and Tom to Iceland the previous June, even Gerry took notice. "I really feel like your mother's ill," he suggested. "She needs some help." I agreed, but I didn't know how to raise the issue with her at the time. Then, after Gerry died, my mom had her own major breakdown and was hospitalized briefly while I was in Aruba. I couldn't call on her for help now. Tom, who had been my lifeline in the immediate aftermath of Gerry's death, was now fully occupied—along with my sister, Kim—supporting my mother.

I didn't want to reach out to other members of my close-family-and-friend circle, either. I was too ashamed. But somehow, my aunt Debbie, my father's twin, found out, as did my cousin Haley and my friends, Anne, Aly and Lesley. They all showed up at the hospital to support me. Haley dropped off one of her housecoats, my pyjamas and the wedding album, even a paint-by-number set I'd been working on before I was hospitalized.

But in the beginning, it was just Tanya. She spent the first day with me in the hospital hallway. Mostly, I guess, I slept. When I did get up to try to go to the bathroom, Tanya told me later, I stumbled down the hall from one wall to the other and back, like a drunk. "I was worried you weren't going to be able to make it back from the bathroom," she said.

At some point, a young-looking psychiatrist came to talk with me. "How are you feeling?" the doctor asked.

"I'm pissed off I'm still alive," I told him, adding that if he would only let me out, I'd go home and try again.

He admitted me to the short-stay psychiatric unit instead.

"THIS IS FOR YOU," she said softly, handing me her drawing, a pencil-doodled circle of flowers with a printed-out poem on lined paper pasted in the middle of the page.

> *Farmers will burn their fields*
> *completely bare in order to provide*
> *the next crop with maximum growth*
> *Just because you've turned to ash*
> *Does not mean you can't bounce back.*

Her name was Rachel, and in one of those odd twists of life— they say you meet the people you need when you need them—we bonded over our shared pain. I didn't tell her much. I told her my husband had died, and she said, "My friends died." I learned later that two of her friends had been hit by a train; a third died by suicide. By mutual unspoken agreement, we decided to sit together in our sadness at a table in the middle of the short-stay unit. Even though Rachel always dressed in her jeans and I wore the housecoat Haley had brought me, I thought of us as "friends in housecoats."

The short-stay psychiatric unit was just a big room with perhaps a half a dozen beds at the far end, each with only a curtain for privacy. Not that that offered any privacy. You could hear people crying—I would have been among them—or arguing with the nurses or yelling about stuff only they understood. Seeing how truly troubled some of my fellow patients were gave me the opportunity to put my own situation in perspective. I wasn't crazy. I was just sad—really, really sad. *I shouldn't even be here*, I thought. I could have checked myself out; I'd admitted myself voluntarily. But I also knew that if I did leave, I wouldn't have access to medication or follow-up treatment, and, while I might not be crazy—my word for the kind of serious mental illness I saw all around me—I knew enough to know I needed help.

The nurses' station was at the opposite end of the room, at the entrance to the ward, and in between there were a few couches and a TV, along with a table where patients could eat their meals or do crafts.

Rachel and I spent a lot of time together at that table. Rachel was in her twenties, younger than me, but also the only woman close to my age in the unit at the time. She was so thin and fragile, she reminded me of a porcelain teacup; if you dropped her, she would shatter. Her parents came every day to have lunch with her, and they would talk with me, too.

The rest of the time, Rachel would draw—she was talented—while I worked beside her on my paint-by-numbers. Since Gerry died, I'd taken up adult paint-by-numbers and piano lessons just to help distract myself from the life I was living. I'd played piano as a kid and had always dreamed of playing again. Before he died, in fact, good old dream-fulfilling Gerry had encouraged me to buy a piano. I did, but I didn't begin playing again until after he died, and I needed something, anything that would bring me joy, which it did. So did painting. Even filling in designated colours on a large, complex canvas had become another lifeline for me, one of the few opportunities I had to block out the life noise all around me and just focus on each small task, adding each bit of paint in its proper place.

At one point, while we sat together at the table, painting, I told Rachel I felt like I had nothing, that everything I cared about was gone. Later, she handed me her drawing with the poem. *Just because you've turned to ash / Does not mean you can't bounce back.* I still have it. I framed it, and I keep it on my wall to remind myself.

I'm not sure now if I even said goodbye when I left. I know we exchanged numbers, and I did text her a week later, just to check in on her. "I'm OK. Hope you are too." She texted back that she was. We never talked again after that. But in that place and time, she helped me. And I hope I helped her, too.

"SO, HOW ARE you feeling now?"

It was Tuesday morning, a full week after I'd arrived at the hospital in an ambulance. I was seated at one end of a rectangular table where the team—the head psychiatrist, a social worker, three or four psychologists—would decide my next steps.

The short-stay psychiatric unit is intended for patients in crisis who are admitted for up to seventy-two hours, stabilized and evaluated and the course of their future care is determined. But because I arrived at the beginning of a long Easter weekend, when only a skeleton staff was on duty, I couldn't meet with the psychiatric team until after the holiday. By then, I desperately wanted to be home in my own bed, in my own house, again.

First thing that morning, I'd gone to the nurses' station near tears. "I really want to go home," I said. "Can I please see the team today?"

"I'll see what I can do," the nurse answered. And she did. I was the first person they met with that day.

For some reason, I'd assumed I would be treated badly, perhaps because I was on a mental health ward and had tried to kill myself, but the nurses were amazing, friendly, empathetic, respectful. "No one here was surprised when we saw your file land on our desk," one nurse confided. They made it seem as if they understood the pain I'd been going through and the reasons why I'd done what I'd done.

The team in front of me now was just as empathetic. "You've been through quite a trauma," Greg Lambert, the social worker, told me. "Your response wasn't outside the realm of normal, so don't feel ashamed. Many people would have felt the same way."

As for me, I no longer wanted another chance to kill myself. "I'm grateful for everything," I said in reply to the question about how I was feeling, "and I'd like to go home."

TANYA HAD CALLED Richard to let him know I was in the hospital. Richard then informed the trustee, without explaining why or disclosing any of the details. I still hadn't formally signed the asset preservation documents. When I told Richard I might be in the hospital for a week, he seemed doubtful. "OK," he said finally. "I think the trustee will be understanding to a point, but—"

To a point! I wanted to scream. I'm in the hospital after having tried to kill myself, and the trustee can't wait a couple of days for me to sign a few more documents?

WHAT IF GERRY really was a bad person? Did I love a bad person? If I did, did that make me a bad person, too? Those questions had been haunting me since the day I answered Richard's call in Aruba. While I waited for an appointment to see the psychiatrist, I tried to find a private-practice psychologist I could talk to. A few turned me down flat. "Have you attempted suicide in the last year?" Yes. "Sorry, we can't help." I did get an appointment with one woman. I was sitting in her office, crying, telling her about how Gerry died on our honeymoon.

"Aww," she said, breezing past what I'd actually told her, "my husband and I just got back from our honeymoon, too."

Finally, Greg Lambert, the social worker I'd met in the short-stay unit, called to check in on me. I told him I hadn't been able to find anyone to help.

"You come in," he responded immediately. "You need to talk to somebody."

And so I did. Greg met me in the hospital lobby, and we found an unused office to just sit and talk. I started meeting with him every few weeks, for an hour or so, in whatever empty room he could find.

Greg was different than anyone else I talked to. The psychologists I'd seen had an annoying, unhelpful habit of saying things like "So, what you're telling me is that you're sad." I didn't need someone to tell me what I'd already told them. Greg, on the other hand, would respond like a real person. "That sucks," he'd say. "That really sucks."

It felt good to have someone else say it out loud. Because by then, I was totally confused. *Did Gerry really die?* "Of course he died," Greg said. "You were there." I was, but even I had begun to doubt the evidence of my eyes. I needed Greg to ground me in reality again, in common sense.

Greg gave me the confidence to finally ask the question I'd been afraid to ask, to confront the demon nagging at my head and my heart. In the months since he died, I'd kept replaying something Gerry said to me in another context—which I can't even remember now—way back when we were still in Scotland: "Bad things happen to bad people." By contrast, he told me, we were "good people."

The Gerry I knew had been the perfect husband, the best friend and one of the kindest and most loving people I'd ever met.

Even as the evidence piled up daily in front of me of another, secretive, manipulative, deceitful, even criminal Gerry, I clung to the belief he must have had a plan. If he hadn't died, I kept telling myself, Gerry would have been able to take that CIBC money the courts had finally unfrozen, solve Quadriga's cash flow problems, open the cold wallets, ensure the company's investors got what they were owed and make everything right with our world again. I knew now that that wasn't true, "But if Gerry was a bad person, had I loved a bad person?" I asked Greg. "Does that make me a bad person, too?"

Greg looked me in the eye. "Good people," he said simply, "can do bad things."

13

Nothing Fixes Awful

The reality is that the money never mattered to me. I didn't fall in love with Gerry Cotten because of his wealth. When we met, he didn't have that much, at least not by the fairy-tale standards Quadriga would set for us just a few years later. It was a bonus when the value of a single bitcoin rocketed through the roof and Gerry appeared to be making more money than we could possibly spend in a couple of lifetimes. I won't lie: I loved being rich. I loved not having to ask, "Can I afford that?" I could—whatever *that* was. We could buy a house in Nova Scotia, another in British Columbia, even our own island with a yacht— not *just* a sailboat—to get us there. We could travel to exotic places I once would never have imagined adding to my bucket list, fly my friends to the Bahamas in our jet for a weekend getaway, take my mother and stepfather to Paris to celebrate her sixty-fifth birthday. Gerry and I could get married in a castle in Scotland. We could lend my friend Anne and her husband the money they needed to buy their first house. We could decide to underwrite the construction of an orphanage in India because we'd seen a program about it on TV. I imagined the orphanage as a first step on the path to becoming a philanthropist. Being able to do what you wanted when you wanted where you wanted just because you wanted was, without doubt or question, beyond satisfying.

But that wasn't why I fell in love, or stayed in love, or, perhaps especially, *am* still in love with that skinny, blond-haired Gerry I matched with when I swiped right on Tinder back in November 2014. Before he became that other, different Gerry I only discovered through the revelations that followed his death.

In the aftermath of my attempt to kill myself, my mind seemed to fly off the rails in diametrically opposing directions. One moment, I would think, *I've lost the most important thing in my life, so nothing else anyone does to me can matter. Take everything I possess; I don't care.* The next minute, I would ask myself why—having just lost the most important thing in my life—I should now have to lose everything else, too.

By June, I only knew I needed to find a way out of this morass.

Because, as Greg the social worker had so aptly put it, my life as I was living it sucked.

Under the terms of the asset preservation order, which I finally signed off on the day after I left the hospital, I received $10,000 a month. That may seem reasonable—and it might have been—except I had to use that money not only to cover my current living expenses, but also to maintain significant aspects of a lifestyle Gerry and I had lived, but which I could no longer afford and yet—thanks to the court order—couldn't easily dispose of. I was still responsible for the upkeep, insurance, taxes and the rest on our house in Kelowna, for example, but I wasn't permitted to sell it without the trustee's OK. It was another asset I was required to preserve—and pay for—until someone other than me decided what to do with it.

I received the $10,000 a month—before taxes and other deductions—not from the capital of Gerry's estate, as many assumed, but out of Robertson Nova's monthly rental income. I continued to run that business with Tanya and Tom, who were also paid from company revenues.

Our tenants knew what was happening. How could they not? Images of the buildings where they lived were often featured in TV news reports about the latest twists and turns in the Quadriga saga. Later, when we had to begin transferring the properties to the new management company the trustee had chosen, some tenants confided in me about how nervous they were about what the change in ownership might mean for them. I did my best to reassure them, though I had no real idea what was in store for them. Most were understanding, even sympathetic. I wasn't surprised. I'd been careful in building Robertson Nova to buy the right kinds of properties—not luxurious, but well built and then well looked after—in order to attract the kinds of loyal tenants who would be responsible and care for them as well. There were exceptions. A few tenants, taking advantage of the uncertainty, threatened to leave without paying their rent; one actually did. No matter. We—Tom, Tanya and I—had to continue operating Robertson Nova on a business-as-usual basis, even though we all understood we would soon lose our own jobs, too.

When I'd hired Tanya, one of the first tasks I set for her was to create an elaborate Excel spreadsheet to track expenses and finances for Robertson Nova, which she then maintained. We had every receipt and could account for every penny that came in or went out. So, when the trustee demanded to see the company's books, I was able to respond with spreadsheets and documentation. The irony in that was that no one had been able to find evidence Gerry had kept any financial records of any sort for Quadriga. I initially dared to hope this would earn me some of the trustee's confidence, but I don't believe it did. At one point, for example, after a contractor we'd hired to do some work used one of our company credit cards to commit fraud, I immediately cancelled the card and told Richard what had happened. He informed George Kinsman, who wrote back to say this was exactly why they wanted to get me out of the company—"Jennifer doesn't know how to run the company." Really? Someone had committed fraud against the company, and I'd taken action to report it as soon as it was discovered.

I was also still being pilloried regularly in the press and online, and it became worse every time Ernst & Young issued its latest report. The language in the reports themselves always tended to be dry and corporate and qualified:

> The Trustee notes that it appears that corporate and personal boundaries between the Companies, Mr. Cotten, Ms. Robertson and other related parties may not have been maintained. Accordingly, the Trustee continues to assess the Estate's rights and interests in relation to the assets associated with the Asset Preservation Order and/or other transactions which may be identified as being at undervalue or preference payments requiring specific investigation.

But the clear implication was that I'd knowingly been involved in whatever nefarious schemes Gerry had carried out, and I could not be trusted. I asked Richard to ask the trustee to stop referring to our "lavish lifestyle" in their reports—it seemed unnecessary to me—and to at least make it clear how completely I had cooperated with their efforts to get to the bottom of what had happened. He said he would, and he probably did, but it didn't seem to me that anything changed. Along with Gerry, I was the villain of this story.

It only got worse. In early June, the FBI announced it was trying to identify victims of Gerry's fraud to "provide them with information and assistance." According to a news report, "the American investigation includes resources from the Internal Revenue Service, the US Attorney's Office for the District of Columbia and the computer crime section of the federal Justice Department." In a report from the trustee, the FBI investigation became just one of four "independent active law enforcement or regulatory reviews in progress . . . Other agencies requests may subsequently materialize." *Coindesk*, a cryptocoin news site, reported that Australian authorities had even become involved. *Australia?*

Finally, I went to Richard and told him I'd had more than enough. I was ready to write a final ending to this chapter of my life, reach a walk-away settlement with the trustee and try to restart my own life again. At that point, the value of the assets I nominally controlled—all of which were under the asset preservation order—totalled around $12 million. Richard and I talked about how much of that I might be able to keep in a settlement. Not much, Richard said. The reality was, we'd be negotiating not only with the bankruptcy trustee, but also with a committee representing what was described as Quadriga's "affected users' group"—cheated investors who, understandably, wanted to claw back every penny Gerry had ever taken out of Quadriga, legitimately or otherwise. "If it's their money and that's been proven," I told Richard, "then they should have it. It should go back to them."

Robertson Nova? There was not a chance I could keep that. Though the company might bear my name, and though I had worked extremely hard to make it a success, the fact was that it had been launched with Gerry's now-disputed bitcoin casino winnings. I'd acquired each additional property using cash Gerry transferred to me, which I had no idea he had illicitly transferred from Quadriga. So, I would never be allowed to keep my company, or its $5 million in real estate. Losing the company would also mean losing my job, and with it, an opportunity to rebuild my reputation—and my finances.

Kinross? "You can ask for the house," Richard said, "but it's going to be a fight, it's going to take months and it's going to be terrible."

I wasn't sure I could survive that. I didn't care about most of the rest of what we owned. I'd never wanted a yacht or an airplane. I didn't need a house in British Columbia, or an island off Nova Scotia, or even land on a lake in Fall River. That's not to say that having what I'd thought of as mine suddenly taken away from me didn't rankle. Or that I didn't sometimes resent that I was being made to pay the price for Gerry's misdeeds.

Not all of the pennies the affected users wanted back, I pointed out, had come directly from Quadriga, or from Gerry. Sometimes, the path was more complicated. Take my Shopify shares, for example. Early on in our relationship, Gerry introduced me to Questrade, the Canadian online discount brokerage, which he used to buy and sell shares without the need for—or costs of—a stockbroker. He'd set up an account for me and then suggested— he knew far more about investing than I did—which stocks I should buy. I followed his advice, but I also learned for myself what trends to watch for. During my time in the HR department at Travelers, I'd noticed just how many of my recruiting friends were being hired at Shopify, the Ottawa-based e-commerce platform. If they were hiring so many recruiters, I reasoned, it probably meant they were about to expand dramatically. So, I bought some shares. Unlike many of the stocks Gerry had suggested I buy—most of which hadn't generated any significant profit—my shares in Shopify soon went through the roof. "Who's the real brains?" I would taunt Gerry with a laugh. And he would laugh back. It is true that the $45,000 I'd initially used to buy the Shopify stock came from Gerry, but did that make the $100,000 in profits I earned as a result of my investment decision mine? Or did those belong to Quadriga's users, too? The short answer: Quadriga's users got it all.

Richard didn't discourage me from making my case, but he wasn't encouraging, either. "We can fight," he allowed. "It'd probably go on for at least two years in court, and in the media, but you'd probably end up with a little more."

"I don't want to do that," I said emphatically. "I don't want to do that to the users. I don't want to do it to me. I want to live. I just want to be happy again."

In the end, I came up with a number myself. "Tell them I want $120,000, my engagement ring and my wedding band. I want my Jeep. And I want my RRSP." Although my registered retirement savings plan had been lumped in as yet another asset I had to pre-serve, the fact was that I'd been growing it since I was sixteen, all the way through to the end of my time at Travelers Insurance. It still wasn't worth much—maybe $20,000—but I couldn't believe

I should be forced now to negotiate for something that was mine, and always had been, but that was where we were.

"Really?" Richard responded when I told him what I wanted. "Oh, I think they'll agree to that because it's very low."

Richard was wrong about that.

TANYA AND I sat at a table on the outdoor patio at the Lower Deck, a waterside pub overlooking Halifax Harbour, surrounded by happy summer tourists, and nursed our beers. It was a sunny August afternoon, and we were putting in time until my appointment that afternoon with Richard. Another one.

In the months since Gerry died, Tanya had become not just my assistant, but also a pillar of personal and emotional support. Because I was now on various medications and didn't feel safe driving, and Tanya didn't feel comfortable letting me, she had volunteered to ferry me to my various appointments, including today's session with Richard in a nearby office tower. It must not have been easy for Tanya. Many of her friends, she confided, had asked her whether she thought Gerry was alive, whether I knew he was. "If this was all an act," she told me she'd told them, "then Jen is the best actress I have ever seen, because I've never seen a woman in more pain and sadness than her." More often than not, I would get into Tanya's Kia SUV, cry all the way to Richard's office, get out, go up to his office, weep some more, then come down, get back in the car and cry all the way home while Tanya kept her eyes on the road.

I had lots to cry about. The settlement negotiations dragged on, with no end in sight. I was beyond frustrated. "The whole point of me suggesting a really low settlement," I would remind Richard, "was to save them money, save me money, save my peace of mind." I'd expected that, as a result of my willingness to forgo a court fight, everything could be settled quickly and amicably. Instead, it seemed that every aspect of every asset of every sort became one more subject for scrutiny and debate.

Including, perhaps especially, my engagement ring. Whenever I looked at it, I thought of that summer picnic lunch aboard the *Gulliver* when Gerry enticed me out onto the deck, got down on his knees and proposed: "You're my best friend. Will you marry me?" But I now knew that my sentimental attachment to it could never trump what that diamond-encrusted band of precious metal represented for Quadriga's investors. It had been appraised at $80,000. In practical terms, selling it would put only the smallest of dents in the huge losses they'd already suffered. But, symbolically, taking that ring off my finger offered a small measure of vengeance for all that Gerry had done to harm them. I decided not to fight to keep the ring.

In fact, even though we still hadn't reached a final settlement, I had come downtown today to reluctantly turn the ring over to Richard for safekeeping. I say reluctantly, not because I doubted by then that Gerry had used funds he shouldn't have to buy the ring, but because part of me still loved the Gerry I had known before I knew all the rest, and the ring was a symbol of that. But if I somehow lost the ring before the deal was done, I knew the users would see that as further evidence I was the person they already assumed I was. Of course you lost it. Sure, you did. I couldn't have faced that.

Today, I took one last look at my engagement ring sparkling in the sunlight. I tried to remember that better time back on the yacht, back on that other sunny summer afternoon, so recent, back before . . .

"Here," Tanya said, handing me her phone. "These just arrived." We were now in the lobby of Stewart McKelvey's law office, waiting for my meeting with Richard. I took Tanya's phone and saw the photo on her screen. Gerry's bench! Beside the trail, overlooking the lake. Just as I'd imagined it.

Before Gerry and I moved to Nova Scotia, I'd told him about the Red Spruce Loop, a walking trail near our old family cottage.

Growing up, the rustic 4.7-kilometre trail—which meanders over hills dotted with magnificent hemlocks, through a stand of red spruce, past brooks and a mossy bog before snaking back to its starting point along the Lake Martha shoreline—had been one of my favourite hiking spots. "I can't wait to take you there," I told him. "I hope you love it, too." Gerry did. Though no one would ever have mistaken Gerry for an outdoorsy guy, the park, for some reason, quickly became one of his favourite places on earth. We would often drive the half hour from Kinross to the park, just so we could walk Nitro and Gully around the Loop together.

After Gerry died and before all the controversies erupted, I had tried to think of fitting ways to memorialize him, to make something positive out of this awful negative.

I had spoken with the local branch of the Crohn's and Colitis Foundation, for example, about making Gerry the face of the organization's upcoming annual Gutsy Walk fundraiser. Initially, they were keen. My friend Aly, the journalist, prepared a write-up, and I contributed one of our engagement photos. The foundation had already posted them on their website when all the Quadriga shit hit the fan.

Not long after, the Canadian head of the foundation called me. She was lovely and gently tried to frame the issue in terms of what was best for me. "If your husband is the focus of the walk," she explained, "you would be expected to make a lot of media appearances. I don't know if you want to do that right now."

I didn't. I also didn't want to drag the foundation into the media mess Gerry's life had become. "You know what," I answered, "my only goals were to raise money and spread awareness of the disease. What I want is whatever is best for the organization, so, if having Gerry as the public face of the walk won't help achieve those goals, then let's not do that."

The foundation quickly removed all traces of Gerry from its website.

But the managers of a nearby historical attraction and park expressed no such qualms when I offered to donate a bench for walkers along a local trail. Although it had taken longer than expected for the handcrafted red spruce wooden bench I commissioned to be completed and installed, it finally was ready. The park's manager texted the photographic proof to Tanya, who'd handled most of the arrangements and now passed on the photos to me. The photos showed the bench in a small clearing overlooking a lake. The simple inscription burned into the top board read:

FOR G

LOVE ALWAYS: J, N & G

[Jennifer, Nitro and Gully]

WE WILL ALWAYS BE

TOGETHER IN OUR FAVOURITE SPOT

I couldn't help but smile. And then I cried.

I WAS STILL having nightmares. Real. Vivid. Frightening. Gerry had done something to hurt me, like having an affair or lying, and I'd caught him in his lie, and the pain was visceral, almost physical. Or we'd be someplace I've never been, and Gerry was dying and needed some very specific medicine. I would run all over town, desperately looking for what he needed, but never find it and never get back in time to save him before he died. It was always my fault. Or Gerry would be talking to me as he normally would, but his face would be blue—that same dark, frozen blue it had been in death. To make matters worse, the nightmares didn't go away after I woke up; echoes of them would haunt my thoughts all day. Being awake was worse. I now knew I was staring into a real-life abyss: no home, no job, no Gerry, no life beyond this awful moment.

"It's like you're trying to swim, but you're just treading water," the psychiatrist told me. "And if we don't do something, you're going to drown." That something was medication.

I'd finally begun seeing Dr. William Wood, a well-respected local psychiatrist, in May as I tried to deal with all the changes happening in my life and in my head. I was still seeing him in September as my mental health deteriorated and the negotiations for the settlement ground on.

Even before I had such good reasons to be, I'd been an anxious person—a people-pleasing overachiever who couldn't take criticism and worried that her best was never good enough. Before Gerry died, I'd been on Zoloft, an antidepressant, mostly to level out my emotions. I experienced one of its side effects: crazy dreams, which morphed into nightmares as soon as Gerry died. I couldn't cope, so I stopped taking Zoloft cold turkey. But the nightmares didn't stop.

My family doctor then prescribed Ativan before bedtime to help me sleep. It didn't. She tried clonazepam, a sister drug, which was supposed to be effective longer. It wasn't. So, I went back on Ativan, but the dosage—half a milligram twice a day—still wasn't enough to allow me to deal with my life.

Dr. Wood had upped my Ativan dosage—to one milligram four times a day—but he also prescribed another drug called prazosin, an alpha blocker used to control nightmares in people with post-traumatic stress disorder. It worked. Finally. I still dreamed, but those dreams became fewer and less vivid and upsetting.

Not that life got any easier. It was late September, and I was now back in Dr. Wood's office, still crying.

"I wish I could give you even more medicine," he said finally, "but nothing fixes awful."

THE FINAL TERMS of the settlement were made public on October 7, 2019—the day before what would have been Gerry's and my first wedding anniversary—in the "Fourth Report of the Trustee."

I agreed to personally transfer to the trustee my "right, title and interest in all assets including cash, investments, vehicles, loans (and related security), real estate (including the Kinross Property, which is to be vacated by October 31, 2019), personal belongings, and any further assets identified in the future." The estate of which I was still theoretically the executor agreed to turn over the same, along with "all boats, planes and cars." Tom had to hand in the keys to 2017 Toyota Tacoma Gerry had bought for him.

In exchange, I got to keep what the agreement referred to as "excluded assets": $90,000 in cash; my $20,000 RSP; my 2015

Jeep Cherokee, with a book value of $19,000; my jewellery—including my wedding band and a pink sapphire ring I'd bought in Greece, valued at $8,700, but not my engagement ring—personal furnishings up to a value of $15,000; and my "clothing and similar personal effects."

The trustee justified its decision to "give" me that much because "the estimated aggregate net realizable value of the excluded assets is likely less than the costs that would have been incurred in pursuing the trustee's claims against Ms. Robertson, the estate and the controlled entities." In other words, it was cheaper for them to settle than to pay lawyers to fight me in court. My own lawyer put it another way: given that the assets I turned over were estimated to be worth $12 million, I'd ended up with slightly more than one percent of the total value of the assets.

I didn't care. Not about the money itself. But I did want Quadriga's investors—some of whom I knew had lost their life savings and were legitimately angry—to understand not only that I had not been a party to Gerry's schemes, but also that I'd cooperated with the monitor and the trustee throughout the entire process to ensure that they were treated as fairly as possible.

I asked Richard to ask the trustee to include words to that effect in its report. The trustee said no, but added I should feel free to write my own statement reflecting that. And so I did:

Following the sudden and unexpected death of my husband, Gerald (Gerry) Cotten, I made every effort to assist in the recovery of QuadrigaCX assets for the benefit of affected users. Using money I then thought was properly mine, I provided the initial funding necessary to enable the [creditor protection] process and agreed to act as a director of the companies so that the CCAA process could proceed.

Since the initiation of the CCAA proceeding, and as outlined in the monitor/trustee's reports, I have been responsive, helpful, and cooperative with the monitor/trustee in the search for and recovery of cryptocurrency and other QCX assets. In April, I voluntarily committed to preserving the assets of my late husband's estate and my own personal assets to ensure future protection for the affected users should that be required.

I have now entered into a voluntary settlement agreement where the vast majority of my assets and all of the estate's assets are being returned to QCX to benefit the affected users. These assets originally came from QCX at the direction of Gerry.

As I have indicated throughout this proceeding, I

had no direct knowledge of how Gerry operated the business prior to his death and was not aware of his improper actions in managing the QuadrigaCX business as outlined by the monitor in its fifth report in June. Specifically, I was not aware of nor participated in Gerry's trading activities, nor his appropriation of the affected users' funds.

As a result of the monitor's investigation, I have agreed to return to QCX assets that I had previously thought were purchased with Gerry's legitimately earned profits, salary, and dividends.

I was upset and disappointed with Gerry's activities as uncovered by the investigation when I first learned of them and continue to be as we conclude this settlement.

I believe this settlement is a fair and equitable resolution for QCX and the affected users, which lets the Trustee continue to do the business of recovering as much as possible for the affected users in an efficient way that keeps trustee and legal fees as low as possible going forward. In return, this settlement will allow me to move on with the next chapter of my life.

I only wished that last sentence could be true.

* * *

LATER IN THE FALL of 2019, I found myself in a boardroom in downtown Halifax, explaining one more time everything that happened in that ICU in Jaipur on the day Gerry died—reliving the horror, retelling it all again for yet another group of strangers.

"I need a moment," I blurted suddenly to the room full of lawyers and investigators. I was having a panic attack. I felt like I was about to pass out. I got up and ran out of the room.

On this day, the questions were coming from investigators for the Ontario Securities Commission [OSC], which had launched its own investigation into Quadriga. Everyone, it seemed, still had questions for me—often the same ones, over and over.

Under the terms of my settlement agreement, I had agreed to be "examined under oath" by the trustee. That swallowed a whole afternoon. *Do you know this company? Do you know that company?* What I knew was that most of the companies they asked me about had strange names, and I'd never heard of any of them. I wanted to reply, "Why are you asking me about them?" But I didn't. My guess is that they were just getting me on the record as saying I didn't know anything about all sorts of companies that had had some connection to Quadriga in case they later discovered I did know, in which case they could come after me for lying. I wasn't lying; I didn't know anything. But I had the distinct impression everyone still assumed I must be hiding some money somewhere.

I'd also spent a full day answering questions from the Canada Revenue Agency (CRA). It was conducting what it called a "lifestyle audit," trying to match up what I'd earned and what I'd spent to determine if I'd reported everything I was supposed to. I had. I'd prepared my own personal taxes, and they were complete. Gerry had promised to file Robertson Nova's corporate taxes for 2017, but hadn't. I knew at the time he was stressed about CIBC, so I didn't press him. "Don't worry," he said, "I'll get to it," adding that simply filing the return late wasn't such a big deal. "There might be a minor fee or something," he'd said. And then he was dead, and here I was.

When did you buy this vehicle? That property? How much did you pay? All of the information was already in the public record, of course, and I no longer owned any of what the CRA officials were asking me about. At one point, I turned to Richard. "Why do I have to answer all these questions if I don't even own them anymore?" But he said I did. And so I did.

Now it was the OSC's turn. It had sent a lawyer and an investigator from Ontario to question me. Richard accompanied me to the session, which lasted all day. A woman from the Nova Scotia Securities Commission sat in on the interview, too, but it was the delegation from Ontario who grilled me relentlessly, questioning me in agonizing detail about everything, including how

Gerry died—or *if* he did. The OSC, along with interviewers for the trustee and the Nova Scotia Securities Commission, became obsessed with the theory that Gerry might have faked his death and was now hiding somewhere. They even kept circling back to questions about Gerry's fascination with Japan. "You're not going to find him in Japan," I told them. "He's dead."

Finally, I snapped, bolted out of the room and went into a bathroom, where I threw up. I ended up sitting on the bathroom floor, crying. I don't know how long I was there, but the woman from the Nova Scotia Securities Commission eventually came to check on me. She was very caring, and I was eventually able to continue. I think everyone felt badly that I'd been so traumatized, but that didn't stop them from asking even more questions.

Although I survived all those interrogations, I still wasn't allowed to finally close the book on the Quadriga chapter of my life. As part of the settlement, I had also agreed to work with the trustee to file a motion in a court in California to obtain data from Google. Under California law, it would have been almost impossible for the trustee to get access to Gerry's Google account without my OK as his executor. I was happy to oblige, though the process dragged on for even more months. In the end, I have no idea what, if anything, they discovered. No one told me.

* * *

"THERE ARE NO van Goghs here," I said, trying to make a joke and keep the tone light, but the man rifling through my belongings seemed not to see the humour. Truthfully, neither did I.

Under the terms of the settlement, I had been allowed to keep $15,000 worth of furnishings. "Should we fight that?" I'd asked Richard during the negotiations. No need, he said. That amount should more than cover my household furniture. He was right. But before I could move my belongings out of Kinross, the trustee had insisted that an appraiser evaluate everything, just to be sure. The appraiser himself was a lovely man; the Ernst & Young representative who accompanied him not so much.

He rooted through my drawers, bins and closets, examined my personal items, trying to find anything worth something. He'd point out items to the appraiser. "Take a picture of this . . . Take a picture of that." Finally, he opened a closet door and discovered a large framed provincial government map of Little Island, the South Shore property where Gerry and I had planned to build our getaway.

"This belongs to the property," he said, sounding triumphant.

"No, it doesn't," I insisted. "My friend Anne gave it to me as a Christmas gift the year before Gerry died. So, first of all, it doesn't belong to the property. And second of all, it's not worth anything to sell." I was crying. Again. Still. It was all so degrading.

"Whatever," I said finally. "Take it. Keep it for Little Island." And he did.

Once they'd completed their appraisal, I had less than two weeks to pack up my life at Kinross and move out for good. On October 31, 2019, I took one final walk-through of every room in my now-empty house that was no longer mine, recalling a moment here, savouring a memory there. And then I left before the first of the Halloween trick-or-treaters could begin their rounds.

Halloween had always been a special night for Gerry. He would buy the biggest, best chocolate bars and hand them out, along with loonies, to the boys and girls who came to the door. He loved seeing—and commenting on—all the kids in their costumes. The year before, one had shown up at our door dressed as Donald Trump. Gerry thought the real Donald Trump was a terrible political leader, but he loved the kid's ingenuity.

Now, as I drove away, I looked in the rear-view mirror at the house, our house, one more time. How many times had I driven away from that house and glanced back, thinking, *That's my house! I love my house!* I knew this would be the last time. And that was just so fucking sad.

THAT WAS THE END. But it wasn't the end. Perhaps there will never be an end.

In December, the Toronto law firm representing the Quadriga users' group sent a letter to the RCMP, asking it to exhume Gerry's body and perform a post-mortem autopsy to confirm his "identity and the cause of death given the questionable circumstances surrounding Mr. Cotten's death and the significant losses of affected users." I only found out about this when a reporter called to ask for my response.

Some people didn't even need an autopsy. In its December issue, *Vanity Fair* magazine published an article entitled "Ponzi Schemes, Private Yachts, and a Missing $250 Million in Crypto: The Strange Tale of Quadriga." Noting that the case was still under investigation by international law enforcement, the magazine told its 1.25 million subscribers that "anonymous accounts posting on Twitter, Reddit, Pastebin, and Telegram" had conducted the "most effective and thorough investigation" of what happened at Quadriga. Their findings, reported the magazine, "could be distilled to a two-word conclusion: Gerry's alive."

It would never end.

14

Follow Your Dreams

What next? What now? I'd been trying to figure out the first stuttering steps into whatever my new life would be ever since Richard and I made our initial settlement proposal to the trustee and the Quadriga users' group back in June.

First things first: I knew I would need to find a new place to live. I briefly imagined trying to negotiate a mortgage to allow me to stay in Kinross, but it didn't take more than a few seconds of contemplation to conclude that would be a non-starter. How could I even pay the property taxes, let alone get a mortgage on a $500,000 house if I didn't have a job? And how could I get a job with all the negative publicity still swirling around me? Would any company hire an HR specialist, a job in which trust is essential, if that person had been accused—even falsely—of masterminding a fraudulent exit scam, or worse, murder? Even if I did manage to land a position, how would I juggle the continuing demands on my time—there always seemed to be more consultations with Richard, more sit-downs with investigators, more documents to sign—with the responsibilities of a nine-to-five position and a new employer's expectations? And was I ready, emotionally, to get up each morning, do my hair, put on makeup, dress in my best business attire and be back in the workforce with a ready smile? I wasn't.

Back to finding a place to live. An apartment in the city? With two dogs? Even if I could find a pet-friendly rental, did I want to commit to a year's lease on accommodation in Nova Scotia when I wasn't sure I wanted to still be in the city a year from now? But if not here, where would I go? Perhaps I was being paranoid, but I couldn't imagine there were many places left in the world where no one had heard of Quadriga or its infamous and nefarious bitcoin widow.

Travel? That still appealed to me—I'd love to return to a pre-Quadriga future of backpacking and hostels! I didn't have to fly first class or stay in a fancy hotel. But I would still need money. While I had walked away from the settlement with a modest amount, it seemed foolish to dissipate all of it on travel without at least a backup job to return to, even one that might simply allow me to earn enough money to keep travelling—forever, if possible. Perhaps I could travel and teach. When I graduated from university, many people I knew flew off to Korea or Japan or China to teach English to children in schools there. Me? I'd married Jacob and started my career in HR. Could I rewind now? Start over almost a decade later? But I had no formal teacher training. I'd never taught. And, having grown up as our family's much younger last child—seventeen years younger than Kim, fourteen than Adam—I'd had no real experience being around children. Should I go back to school now, perhaps train to teach English as a second language? But was I prepared to be in an actual classroom again, to answer questions from teachers and fellow students about what I'd been doing for the past five years? Maybe I could enrol in an online program. But I would still need time to find, apply to and be accepted into such a program.

It sometimes felt like I was locked in an endless thought loop. Back to finding a place to live.

The answer turned out to be much simpler and closer to home than I'd imagined: our family cottage! After my parents split, my father moved there full time and had been slowly renovating it. During a storm a few years earlier, a tree had fallen on its roof.

Since the insurance company agreed to pay to replace the roof, my dad decided he'd go the extra step and frame in a loft, which he planned to leave unfinished until he could afford to complete the work. Gerry had been skeptical. Why bother to pay to add a loft you couldn't use? Then, during the construction, my father fell off the roof. He ended up in the emergency room with a concussion and three broken ribs and had to have surgery on his collarbone, confirming all Gerry's doubts. "This was such a bad idea," he told me at the time.

But now, suddenly, it all seemed like a very good idea to me. The cottage—as far as you can get from the whirl of luxury, exotic travel, yachts and the private jet for which I had become infamous—was familiar, safe. I'd spent a few years of my childhood living there full time. I talked with my father, offering to use some of my settlement money to complete his renovations in exchange for rent-free accommodation. He agreed. So, I designed it and hired contractors I'd worked with at Robertson Nova to insulate and close in the space, add a wall to create a separate bedroom and living area, even squeeze in a small kitchen and bathroom. My stepdad and a friend installed new flooring, and my dad helped with the painting. Together, we transformed the shell of a loft into a cozy, self-contained space where I could live. The loft— just thirty-two feet by twenty-two feet all in—wasn't much bigger than Kinross's combined living room and dining room. In fact, I had to rent a storage unit—ironically, in the same Bedford facility Gerry had once secretly used—to house most of my Kinross furnishings. The only pieces I could fit into the loft were my bed, a set of drawers we'd kept in a hallway at Fall River, our two-person rec room couch, my piano, Gerry's office desk, a computer chair and a filing cabinet.

Still, for now, it was all I—and my dogs—needed. For Nitro and Gully, the fact the cottage was on a dirt road on a lake in the middle of the woods was a playtime bonus. For my father, having a finished loft added value to his property. For me, it meant I could live in a place that was safe and secure while I sorted out the rest of my life. If I did decide I wanted to travel, the cottage could serve as my home base. I could store some of my belongings and know they'd be here when I returned. *If* I returned.

It all felt temporary, and it was—a stopgap measure until I could get back on my feet. But by the beginning of November, when I finally moved in, I was already well into the process of attempting to do exactly that. Something awful might have happened to me, but I was not going to let it ruin—or define—the rest of my life.

* * *

I HOLD UP my handwritten TEACHER JENNIFER sign and wave my hands in front of my face in a cheerfully animated greeting for the smiling little boy staring back at me from the other side of my computer screen, on the other side of the real world. Showtime!

It may be four in the morning in my Atlantic time zone, but it is four in the afternoon in China. No matter how distressing my day before has been, or how much worse I expect the rest of this day to be, I have learned to paste on my happy face and ramp up my theatrical stage presence. I've always been good at compartmentalizing, at focusing on the immediate tasks ahead of me instead of becoming distracted by all those many things I can't control. In the days after Aruba, as the true scale of Gerry's deceptions finally swept over me like a tidal wave, I lost that ability. It only became worse in the immediate aftermath of my suicide attempt, as I struggled with my own questions about my culpability, and in the first, worst days after I realized I was about to lose everything I'd thought was mine.

Greg, the social worker, helped me slowly reframe my thinking. But in the end, what finally allowed me to begin to find my way back to myself again was my own decision to proactively propose a financial settlement I believed would be modest enough to satisfy Quadriga's creditors while allowing me to press the reset button on my life. There have been more than a few hiccups on my road to recovery since then, but I have been busy reclaiming my life one day—and one night—at a time.

Tonight, I've strategically arranged my photographer's backdrop screen—an educational but fun map of the world dotted with hot-air balloons, sailing ships and vintage airplanes—so that my computer camera doesn't take in my unmade bed on the other side of my tiny bedroom. I have laid out tonight's teaching collection of puppets and props within easy reach of my computer, which sits on Gerry's old desk. For some reason, students love my fluffy piggy hat and all-star glasses attire. My goal is to make each twenty-five-minute, one-on-one teaching session so memorable that my student—and, more to the point, my student's parents—will decide to book me again. That's how VIPKid works.

In the decades since 1978, when Chinese leader Deng Xiaoping announced its open-door policy to encourage foreign companies to do business in China, teaching the country's children to speak English has become both a national government priority and also a huge private business opportunity. Although most Chinese children do learn basic English in school, ambitious parents—eager to give their own kids a leg up in life—often invest in private instruction. VIPKid, a Beijing-based company that only launched in 2014—the same year Gerry and I matched on

Tinder—has become one of the most successful online schooling companies. By the time I became a VIPKid teacher in August 2019, the company boasted more than half a million Chinese students who connect over a VIPKid portal with one of more than 60,000 qualified English-speaking teachers, who can be based anywhere in the world.

I am now one of those teachers.

My journey to teaching English to Chinese children in the middle of the night began in June 2019, when I decided to enrol in an eleven-week online program at the Chicago-based International TEFL Academy to earn my Level 5 certificate in teaching English as a foreign language. Although I'd worked as a trainer in some of my HR jobs, I had no idea how to teach—certainly not grammar or phonics, and definitely not to children who didn't understand English. I learned quickly. Despite all the distractions crashing down around me, I did well. I even put the program's instruction to use while I learned, tutoring a sweet young local Chinese boy who lived close to my cousin and had refused to speak English. To my own surprise, I discovered I enjoyed teaching children.

I also began to explore opportunities to teach English to students face to face in Asia. I needed a change of scenery, wanted an opportunity to meet new people. I'd never been to South Korea.

Why not? I asked myself. *Well*, I quickly answered my own question, *because I couldn't just leave. Not yet.* I knew it would take until at least the end of 2019 to extricate myself from all the various legal and business entanglements keeping me tethered to Halifax. In the meantime, I still needed to find a way to make money I could call my own.

A childhood friend recommended that I check out VIPKid. She had become one of its teachers after moving to the United States to marry an American and discovering she wasn't eligible to work there. VIPKid, she told me, offered her the chance to earn income while working remotely, setting her own hours, and the school required no long-term commitment. That seemed to be exactly the kind of short-term opportunity I was looking for, so I applied.

Thanks to my TEFL certification, I had the basic qualifications, although getting hired involved a multi-stage process. I had to record a ten-minute demo class, teaching a pretend student while enthusiastically responding with high fives and feedback like "Great job!" and "Awesome!" if my pretend student got the right answer, and gently, helpfully correcting wrong answers if not. I then had to participate in a live online interview to establish my credentials and show off my teaching approach. No one asked about the rest of my life, and I didn't offer. Later, after studying the school's curriculum and teaching materials and taking a test, I became certified to teach Levels 2 and 3, usually children aged five to twelve who are in the early stages of learning English. By the beginning of August, I was ready to hang out my virtual shingle:

> Hello! My name is Teacher Jennifer and I am so excited to teach you the English language! Classes will be focused on having fun and learning lots! I hold a Bachelor's degree as well as a certificate in Human Resources . . . I have currently completed 180 hours of ESL training through the International TEFL Academy with a focus on young learners . . . I am very patient and love having fun in the classroom. Can't wait to meet you!

That advertisement for myself—translated into Mandarin—as well as a short video showcasing my teaching style and an all-important booking calendar indicating the time slots when I would be available to teach, were all potential students and their parents saw when they went online to choose which classes, and teachers, to sign up for.

At first, I listed myself as being available every night of the week for as many hours as possible, beginning around midnight my time and running through ten the next morning. Some nights, I'd have just one booking; other nights, I might have two or three, but they'd often be spaced out over the entire ten hours—one at 2:30 a.m., another at five o'clock and a third at nine o'clock—so uninterrupted sleep became almost impossible. And then I'd still have to fill my daylight waking hours with demanding meetings or interviews or whatever else I needed to do to inch the final Quadriga settlement along towards its conclusion.

But that crazy schedule—along with positive student reviews—eventually paid off. I began to fill in the empty spaces in my calendar and attract more and more repeat students. Initially, that just made my nights crazier. I'd sometimes teach sixteen straight classes, with just a five-minute break between each. But, after a while—as I became more confident about both my teaching and my ability to attract regular students—I was able to regularize my schedule. These days, I start teaching closer to dawn and end my classes by 10 a.m., which is prime time for students on the other side of the globe.

To increase my universe of potential students, I also got certified to teach at every VIPKid level from one to six, as well as taking specialized training—from beginning grammar and story writing to a variety of science, technology, engineering and math topics—so I could accept more advanced students. That is important, because the more certifications you can claim, the more opportunities you have to attract students; and the more sessions you can teach each month, the more you can earn per session. I now earn about $21 an hour (US). That's pennies compared to what I was taking home as the CEO of Robertson Nova, but my expenses—and my expectations—have changed, too.

Besides, teaching offers plenty of non-monetary satisfactions. With the exception of one three-star rating in my first two weeks of teaching, every review of my teaching since has earned five stars. I am proud of that. Better, there are personal gratifications. The mother of one girl named Shirley—the students get to choose their own English "names"—tells me her daughter has decided she wants only me as her teacher. "Teacher Jennifer, I love you," a boy signs off at the end of every one of our sessions.

Teaching online has also opened fascinating new windows into how other people live, something about which I am still endlessly curious. I'll often catch glimpses of my students' parents, hovering in the background while I teach or even just going about their daily routines while their children learn. One boy, who was eating at his kitchen table during a session, smiled, lifted his chopsticks and held a wonton up close to the screen as if to offer it to me. And, since so many of my students use tablets, they can be almost anywhere during our classes. I've conducted lessons with a student in a park, even at a beach.

Someday, I'd love to travel there, see the country and meet my students in China in person. Someday, I will.

THE TEXT MESSAGE was from my childhood friend Anne, who now lives in Calgary. Back when Gerry and I were rich—it only seems like forever ago—we'd lent Anne and her husband, Alex, money they needed to buy their first house after they discovered Anne was pregnant with their first child. After our own house of Quadriga riches collapsed, they'd had to scramble to renegotiate the loan, since it was considered one more of Gerry's ill-gotten gains that had to be repaid to the creditors.

I hadn't seen them since the previous summer, when I visited Calgary on my way home after packing up the Kelowna house to get it ready to sell. Since I had too many keepsakes and personal items to take on the plane with me, I offered to leave some—including Gerry's winter coat—for their use.

Anne texted me to tell me Alex had just tried on Gerry's coat. He'd reached into the pocket, she wrote, and pulled out handfuls of candy. "We laughed and laughed."

So did I. And then I cried.

* * *

"YOU PROBABLY WON'T remember me," I began my email message to my former professor in early January 2020. I did hope he would remember, and for reasons unrelated to why everyone else seemed to know me these days. During my undergraduate years at Mount Saint Vincent University, I'd taken a number of religious studies courses from him and done very well. I had recently decided to apply to the two-year Bachelor of Education program at the Mount, I explained in my email, and was hoping he'd agree to be one of my academic references. Oh, and by the way, I added, although my last name is now Robertson, I'd gone by Griffith when I was his student.

He quickly wrote back to say he'd looked up my academic record; I'd gotten straight As, so he had no qualms about my abilities or recommending me for the program. "This," he added, "is typically where I ask my students, 'What have you been doing for the last ten years?' But, unless I'm horribly mistaken, your life has been all too public. Are you OK?"

By that point, I was.

After only a few months teaching online, I already knew what I was meant to do in this, my new, next life: teaching! I'd discovered I loved the creativity of shaping a class, of actually teaching and seeing children succeed with my help. Unfortunately, I'd realized this new-found passion too late to apply to the Mount to join the cohort that had begun the teacher training program in September 2019.

While I waited for applications to open for September 2020, I decided I would seek out opportunities to get in-person teaching experience. In the fall, I began tutoring at my local library. Then, at the suggestion of a teacher friend, I volunteered at a local elementary school that was desperate for help teaching English as an additional language to its immigrant students. I worked with the school's resource teacher, offering one-on-one sessions on reading. That led to requests to tutor other students.

It was now mid-March 2020, and I'd just arrived for one such private tutoring session when I saw the email on my phone. It was from Mount Saint Vincent University. The subject line read: "Admissions Information." I didn't want to open it. By then, I'd convinced myself I wouldn't get in. In my head, I ticked off all the logical reasons they would say no: it was a very competitive program, I didn't have much teaching experience, I hadn't taken many relevant courses in my undergraduate program, none of my previous job experience before VIPKid had had anything to do with teaching. Worst of all, I'd submitted my application right on the deadline. I didn't realize until I checked with the admissions office that the department considered qualified applicants on a first-come, first-served basis, meaning my application started its life at the bottom of the pile. I was already considering alternatives. Should I apply to another program somewhere else? Or get more experience and apply again next year? Finally, I opened the email.

> We are pleased to offer you admission to Mount Saint Vincent University. A Bachelor of Education acceptance package will be sent to you within the next 7 to 10 days . . . Congratulations and welcome to the Mount!

The email was dated March 16, 2020.

The day before, the first three cases of coronavirus disease had been diagnosed in Nova Scotia. Within a week, most of the world was in lockdown.

EVEN BEFORE COVID-19, I had come up with a plan—one last thing I wanted to do before I fully embraced my new life, something that would reconnect me with my long-lost dream of becoming involved in international development, something that would further my new goal of becoming a teacher and something that would allow me to write a final ending to this most wonderful/ awful chapter of my life. Full circle.

I wanted, needed, to go back to India.

One of the reasons why Gerry and I travelled to India in December 2018 was to open the orphanage. We never got the opportunity.

My new plan, which had begun to take shape in the first months of 2020, was to return to India for the second anniversary of the orphanage's opening, finally meet its operators and spend a week just helping out, getting to know the children. I'd also made tentative arrangements to travel to the Himalayas for two weeks, live with a local host family and teach English and math in a rural public school to gain practical experience as part of my own teacher training.

My friend Mehek, who had been there with me in some of my worst days after Gerry died, offered to come with me, to be my guide and companion. I couldn't think of anyone better.

While COVID-19 has delayed my plans, it will not derail them. When it is possible again, I will visit the orphanage in Venkatapuram, see the motivational inscription over the entrance that I'd originally written to encourage the children—*Follow your dreams. Reach for the stars. Let your heart be your guide*—and remind myself that those words apply to me, too.

15

Shifting the Colours

What did she know? And when did she know it? Those are the sorts of questions we ask of politicians and public figures. I am not now, nor ever will I be, a politician. I am an accidental, reluctant public figure. I did not seek notoriety. I'm uncomfortable in the spotlight. I only decided to tell my story because so many others presumed to tell it for me and told it incorrectly—and, more often than not, unfairly.

My own answers to those questions?

I didn't know. Not while Gerry was alive. To me, he was a smart, hugely successful businessman working in an innovative area of finance I didn't understand and didn't believe I needed to.

When did I know? It took me longer than many others to

appreciate the extent of Gerry's deceit. Like much of the rest of the world, I learned about Gerry's fraud incrementally, as the first drips of puzzling questions about passwords no one knew and keys to cold wallets no one could find piled on top of emails that promised answers but never arrived. They morphed, at first slowly, then suddenly, into a torrent of doubt that became an inexorable flood of accusation and, finally, a tidal wave of irrefutable evidence that almost swallowed me whole.

You may find this surprising, but part of me still believed with all my heart and most of my head that there would be a different, better answer to all those accusations until that day, in late March 2019, when my lawyer called me in Aruba to inform me investigators had unearthed an unmistakable, undeniable pattern of fraud in Gerry's handling of Quadriga's customers' money.

I get it. I understand the doubts and suspicions. If you simply follow the bread crumbs—from our wedding celebration in Scotland in October 2018, to the signing of our wills less than a month later and just days before we departed on our honeymoon, to Gerry's sudden death in early December in a country far from our home, to his private, closed-casket funeral in Halifax and Quadriga's unfortunate decision to wait a month before announcing his passing—the trail seems to lead inevitably to . . . well, something nefarious. But the reality, as I've tried to explain in this memoir, is far more mundane, random and explicable. All those crumbs put together don't add up to a loaf of truth.

But there is, of course, another, larger question: Should I have known sooner? I don't think so. I was far from the only person Gerry fooled. Before he died, his contractors expressed absolute faith in his leadership and business smarts. In the days after his death was announced, plenty of others he'd worked closely with in the bitcoin industry came forward to attest to his honesty and integrity, and to reassure investors Gerry would not have let them down. And don't forget this: hundreds of thousands of investors trusted Quadriga—and Gerry—with their money. Some did so blindly, often wilfully so. They had been attracted to bitcoin precisely because it operated outside conventional banking's traditional oversight and disclosure guard rails. They trusted Gerry, accepted the risks until they got burned and then they looked around for someone to blame. With Gerry unavailable, many of them chose me.

While there is plenty of blame to parcel out—regulators who didn't regulate, investors who didn't do their due diligence—none of that matters as much as this: "The downfall of crypto asset trading platform Quadriga resulted from a fraud committed by Quadriga's co-founder and CEO Gerald Cotten." That simple, bald statement of fact, which opens the report of the Ontario

Securities Commission's report into the Quadriga collapse, says it all.

> What happened at Quadriga was an old-fashioned fraud wrapped in modern technology. There is nothing new about Ponzi schemes, unauthorized trading with client funds and misappropriation of assets. Crypto asset trading platforms, however, are novel and the regulatory framework for these platforms is evolving. Quadriga did not consider its business to involve securities trading and it did not register with any securities regulator. This lack of registration facilitated Cotten's ability to commit a large-scale fraud without detection. So did the absence of internal oversight over Cotten. From 2016 onwards, Cotten was in sole control of a company that had hundreds of thousands of clients and transacted over a billion dollars of fiat currency–denominated assets and over five million crypto asset units. He ran the business as he saw fit, with no proper system of internal oversight or controls or proper books and records.
>
> Similarly, Quadriga clients could not have known what Cotten was doing. Under the Quadriga busi-

ness model, clients entrusted their money and crypto assets to Quadriga. Quadriga provided no meaningful insight into how those assets were being stored, moved and spent. To the contrary, Quadriga provided false assurances about asset storage. Clients had no means of verifying these claims or obtaining meaningful information about the handling of their assets. This lack of transparency also facilitated Cotten's fraud.

When I first read the report, which was released in June 2020—almost eighteen months after Gerry died and eight months after I'd settled with the trustee—my heart fell to my feet. The OSC not only confirmed what Gerry had done, but also detailed how he had done it and why he had been able to get away with his crimes. As devastating as that was, however, I also began to feel a lightness as I read it, the sense of an enormous weight being lifted from me. It wasn't my fault. I hadn't known anything about Gerry's schemes and played no part in carrying them out. I wasn't the criminal. Gerry was.

But that only raised more troubling questions: Who was Gerry Cotten, the man I loved with all my heart? How do I balance the Gerry I knew in our life together the smartest, funniest, kindest person I'd ever met, a man who taught me so much, the only man

I'd ever known who offered me unconditional love, who made me feel like his number one person always—with the deceitful, manipulative, criminal Gerry who appears in the pages of that report?

I can't. Gerry was intelligent and talented enough to succeed at whatever he turned his mind to. He didn't need to do those terrible things I now know he did. Was it simply—and simple—greed, the sense that even too much was never enough? Or was there something deeper, darker, lurking within, a character flaw that nothing and no one could have fixed?

I don't know, but I can't understand it. I can't imagine stealing even five dollars from someone else. People sometimes ask me, in a joking way but often with serious intent, if I have a stash of cash hidden somewhere. No one in their right mind, they seem to be saying, would simply give up everything. But I did. And I'm glad I did. As much as my life now sucks in comparison with the millionaire's life I led with Gerry—I have a dent in my car I can't afford to fix, I look for bargains every day in the supermarket aisles, I work through the night so I can afford to attend university in the day—I can look myself in the mirror and know I've done nothing wrong.

How did Gerry seem so blasé? I'd give anything to have ten minutes with him today to ask him how the person he was to me did those things he did to so many others. Did he have a plan, some way he intended to make it all right for everyone again? I still want to believe that, but I don't. Not really. Not anymore. Mostly, I just want to ask him why. Why? Why? Why?

Do I have regrets? Of course I do. I regret every awful moment of every day of the terrible year that followed Gerry's death. I regret that I may have lost forever the possibility of living that ordinary extraordinary life I imagined back in high school. I certainly regret that I didn't know what I didn't know long before I knew it. I regret the losses Quadriga investors suffered because of Gerry.

But do I regret having met Gerry? That's a different, more complex question. When we met, I was struggling emotionally and financially, in the aftermath of the collapse of my marriage to Jacob. I needed someone who put me at the centre of his world, who centred my own life, who offered me love and the promise of a shared future together. Gerry did all of that. While I deeply regret how it all turned out—and why it turned out as it did—I can't regret having met Gerry or the love we gave each other in the years we had together.

Do I still love Gerry? Yes, I'll always love him, or at least the him that I knew. I've had two relationships since Gerry died, both with men I met through friends. They each lasted about six months, and neither ended well. In part, that was because they understood I still had feelings for Gerry.

"How can you?" they would ask.

How could I not? "Feelings," I answered, "are complex." And they are. Even my memories of Gerry—the best memories of my life—are tainted by what he did. I will carry with me the disappointment of what I now know Gerry did for the rest of my life.

In the seven years since I swiped right and met Gerry, I have learned that life can be unbelievably joyous, full of adventure, love and curiosity, but it can also bring great sadness, heartbreak and disillusionment. I have discovered many versions of myself, and some I like more than others, but in the end, they are all pieces of me that form one image—one image always changing. My life has been a kaleidoscope. The colours vary, the pieces shift and move, creating new images. I have shifted, too, and changed my colours. Sometimes, I have had to twist the end of the kaleidoscope to rearrange the pieces into an image that would remind me of who I am. Do we ever see the same pieces and colours?

And yet, there are certain verities. Before you can save yourself, you have to love yourself, love all your colours and shapes and the images you create. If you don't, you won't see the beauty anywhere else. There was a time when I believed my life should have ended when Gerry's did. I touched bottom that night in April 2019 in my bedroom, with the wine and the Ativan and the wedding album, convinced that ending my life must be a better option than getting on with it. But then, with the help of words that, when said aloud, sound like clichés and bromides—*Good people can do bad things . . . Bad things happen to good people . . . Your life belongs to you . . . Only you can live your life*—I began to push my way back to the surface, back to me.

I am, I have come to realize, a hopeless romantic, someone who loves to be in love and to be loved, to have a partner in my life. I have reached an age where all my friends are married, or getting married, becoming pregnant, beginning families. I want those things, too. Even after Gerry—not to mention after Jacob and the two others who came after Gerry—I am not about to give up on the possibilities of finding love. I am an eternal optimist.

Perhaps paradoxically, I am also a clear-headed realist, now more determined than ever to never again settle for anything less than defining and controlling my own destiny. I am ready to have a child of my own, to begin the family Gerry was so ambivalent about. I'd prefer to begin that next journey with a man I love, but if I don't find him, that won't stop me. I've been exploring my options. International adoption, I've discovered, is expensive, more than I can afford, and it's difficult for a single woman to jump through all the approval hoops, particularly for anyone like me who has ever been on antidepressants or, perhaps, carries the baggage of my notoriety. But that won't be the end of my quest.

Recently, I made an appointment with a local in-vitro fertilization clinic to explore that possibility. I will find a way. While I don't know what the future holds, I do know I won't allow anyone else to ever again define me or my dreams.

That's also why I've gone back to school—to put myself in control of my destiny. I know I'll never be a millionaire again, but I don't care. My dream—not that far from the one I started with—is still to become a teacher, find a stable job I can call my own, travel to places I've never been, meet someone I can love and be loved by, have a child, start a family and live out my life in a kind of peace I've never known.

I have taken the first step. I am ready for the next steps in my journey.